TO THE ...
H...

XXX OOO XXX
SEPT'09

G000277533

THE COOK'S
POCKET COMPANION

Edited by Jo Swinnerton

PAVILION

A Think Book for Pavilion Books

This edition published by Pavilion Books in 2007
First published in the United Kingdom in 2004 by Robson Books
10 Southcombe Street, London W14 0RA

Imprints of Anova Books Company Ltd

Text and design © Think Publishing 2004
The moral rights of the authors have been asserted

Edited by Jo Swinnerton
The Companion team: Vicky Bamforth, Sarah Bove, James Collins,
Harry Glass, Rhiannon Guy, Annabel Holmes, Emma Jones,
Lou Millward Tait and Malcolm Tait

Think Publishing
The Pall Mall Deposit
124-128 Barlby Road, London W10 6BL
www.thinkpublishing.co.uk

The Soil Association
Registered charity number 206862
0117 914 2447
www.soilassociation.org

All rights reserved. No part of this publication may be reproduced,
stored in a retrieval system, or transmitted in any form or by any
means, electronic, mechanical, photocopying, recording or otherwise,
without the prior permission of the copyright holder.
A CIP catalogue record for this book is available from the
British Library.

ISBN 978-1-862057-90-6

2 4 6 8 10 9 7 5 3 1

Printed by Millenium International Printing, China

The publishers and authors have made every effort to ensure the
accuracy and currency of the information in *The Cook's Pocket
Companion*. Similarly, every effort has been made to contact copyright
holders. We apologise for any unintentional errors or omissions.
The publisher and authors disclaim any liability, loss, injury or
damage incurred as a consequence, directly or indirectly, of the
use and application of the contents of this book.

www.anovabooks.com

THE POCKET COMPANION SERIES:
COLLECT THEM ALL

The Traveller's
Pocket Companion
by Georgina Newbery
and Rhiannon Guy
ISBN 978-1-862057-91-3

The Fishing
Pocket Companion
by Georgina Newbery
and Rhiannon Guy
ISBN 978-1-862057-92-0

The Walker's
Pocket Companion
by Malcolm Tait
ISBN 978-1-862057-93-7

INTRODUCTION

There are some things in life that you simply need to know.

That scientists always recommend the butter be one-seventeenth the thickness of the toast. That a Jerusalem artichoke is neither from Jerusalem nor an artichoke. That cannibals consider the French to be the most delicious and Spaniards barely edible. That to ask for a Duke of York for your Jack The Ripper in a cockney caff is to ask for a fork for your kipper. And that you can't hide a piece of broccoli in a glass of milk.

This little book is no flighty, dippy little fal-de-ral to amuse you in the loo, but a finely crafted, precisely researched, sharply written tomette that just happens to be full of the things you need to know.

You need to know what an anthropophagist eats. What it means to dine with Democritus. Why never to trust a dog to look after your food. That there will always be nine promising ingredients to be found in the cupboard, but that in no combination will they actually make a meal. And that the trouble with eating Italian food is that five or six days later, you're hungry again.

The Cook's Pocket Companion transcends diet regimes, unnatural recipes and tyrannically fashionable ingredients. It is a well-stocked fridge for the mind, ready for leisurely feasting or fast midnight raids.

On a need-to-know basis, this book is more useful than Delia, more stimulating than Jamie and more tempting than Nigella. It has the answers to the questions you have never thought to ask. The perfect companion for people with a hunger for knowledge and a thirst for amusement, it does exactly what good food does: nourish, sustain, and make you feel better.

Jill Dupleix, The Times Cook

SAFETY AT HOME

These are the most common causes of domestic fires in homes in the UK. More than one household in 100 experiences a pan catching fire.

Pan of fat or oil catching fire 24%
Grill pan catching fire 13%
Leaving something in or on the cooker for too long ...7%
Arson..6%
Leaving something too close to the cooker...................5%
Candles...5%
Chimney fires 5%
Toaster..4%
Electric wiring worn out or faulty 3%
Microwave...2%
Cigar/cigarette 2%

COOKING CONUNDRUMS

You have three boxes of fruit. One contains just apples, one contains just oranges, and one contains a mixture of both. Each box is labelled – one says 'apples', one says 'oranges', and one says 'apples and oranges'. However, it is known that none of the boxes are labelled correctly. How can you label the boxes correctly if you are only allowed to take a look at just one piece of fruit from just one of the boxes?
Answer on page 144

HEAD COOK

The word 'lady' means 'bread-maker' or 'kneader of dough' from the old English *hlaefdige*. It was not literal, but was supposed simply to refer to the female head of the household. Similarly, the word 'lord' comes from *hlaford*, meaning 'keeper of bread'.

REASONS TO EAT MORE CHOCOLATE

- Needless to say, many of these things are found in foods other than chocolate without the high levels of sugar and saturated fat. But only a dull person would worry about that.
- Chocolate is high in antioxidants, natural chemicals that help to protect against diseases such as cancer and heart disease. It has nearly twice the antioxidants found in red wine and three times the amount found in green tea
- It is high in flavonoids, which can raise levels of 'good' cholesterol
- It reduces the risk of blood clotting
- It protects against stress on the heart
- It relaxes blood vessels, having a similar effect to mild aspirin and a better effect than red wine
- It contains iron and magnesium
- It contains caffeine, to stimulate
- It contains phenylethylamine, a 'feelgood' chemical that cheers you up

CULINARY LEGENDS

What **Eliza Acton** (1799-1859) really wanted to do was write poetry. But her publisher doubted he could sell a collection of poems by a woman, so he advised her to go away and write a good, sensible cookbook instead. The result was *Modern Cookery for Private Families* (1845) probably the first basic cookbook for the housewife, since cookbooks until then had been written for the trained chef with a full kitchen staff. Eliza spent years testing the recipes, which were well written and easy to understand, and for the first time ingredients were listed separately, rather than in the body of the recipe, which helped to make the book an immediate and long-lasting success.

FILMS FOR FOODIES

American Pie
The Apple
Attack of the Killer Tomatoes
Bread and Roses
Candyman
Chocolat
Coffee and Cigarettes
Cookie
Days of Wine and Rose
Fortune Cookie
The Grapes of Wrath
The Honeytrap
M*A*S*H
Mystic Pizza
The Silence of the Lambs
Spiceworld

THE DELIA EFFECT

In the 1970s, TV chef Delia Smith recommended a particular type of lemon zester on her show, which not only boosted the sales of that implement but also added a new phrase to the English lexicon: 'doing a Delia'. In 1995, Delia used cranberries in a recipe and sales leapt by 200%. In 1998, she demonstrated, to the derision of her fellow chefs, how to cook an egg. In the six weeks that followed, sales of fresh eggs rose by 58 million. When she also recommended her favourite omelette pan, sales leapt from 200 a year to 90,000 in four months. Sales of prunes, Maldon Crystal Salt Flakes, sunblush tomatoes and skewers (for testing cakes) rocketed after a mention on the show. But in 2003 she received the ultimate accolade: the *Collins English Dictionary* listed 'a Delia dish' among its entries, which preserved her place in our culinary culture.

HEATH ROBINSON MAKES A PANCAKE

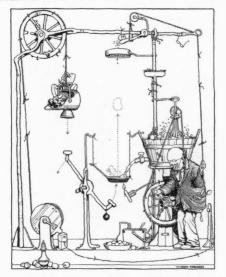

Professor Branestawm's Pancake Machine illustrated
by William Heath Robinson

FUEL FOR THE FIRE

The Great Fire of London took on a culinary theme when
it was alleged to have started in Master Farriner's bakery
in Pudding Lane. It began on Sunday morning, 2
September 1666, and within five days had destroyed
property over 460 acres, including 86 churches. It was
finally brought to a halt by the blowing up of houses at
Pie Corner in Smithfield.

SPOILT FOR CHOICE

This is just a handful of the thousands of varieties of English apple that exist. So if all you get at your local store is Golden Delicious, make friends with your local fruit farm:

Blenheim Orange
Christmas Pearmain
Cornish Gillflower
Crimson Beauty of Bath
Chelmsford Wonder
Chivers Delight
Cornish Aromatic
Crawley Beauty
Easter Orange
Falstaff
Greensleeves
Hawthornden
Hoary Morning

Histon Favourite
King of the Pippins
Michaelmas Red
May Queen
Merton Prolific
Nanny
Nutmeg Pipping
Peasgood's Nonsuch
Pig's Nose Pippin
Rosemary Russet
St Edmund's Russet
Tydeman's Late Orange
Worcester Pearmain

TEN FOODS TO FOOL YOU

Bombay duck is a northern Indian fish dish
Glamorgan sausages are sausage-shaped, but made with cheese
A **Jerusalem artichoke** is neither from Jerusalem nor an artichoke. It's an edible tuber from North America
A **peanut** is not a nut, it's a legume
Mock turtle soup is made with calf's head, beef and veal
A **Salisbury steak** is a hamburger
American coffee cake is a cake, but may not contain coffee; it refers to any cake made to be eaten with a cup of coffee
Poor man's caviar is made of aubergines
Scotch woodcock is anchovies and eggs on toast
Boston crab is a wrestling manoeuvre

FABULOUS FLAPJACK

A piece of flapjack was invented in 2003 that could well revolutionise the diagnosis of several fatal diseases. The supersnack was devised by researchers at the University of Dundee with the help of Alan Clark, the owner of a family-run bakery in the city. Each flapjack contains a small amount of tracer – the naturally occurring stable isotope of carbon – which can be detected by a breath test after it has been eaten. Doctors can then detect whether and how quickly the cake has been absorbed into the patient's system, which can indicate whether a patient is suffering from a bowel disorder, which impairs the digestion of medication used to treat diabetes, irritable bowel syndrome and Aids. The new flapjack method could become a widespread alternative to using radio-active tracers, and would be much tastier.

COOKING CONUNDRUMS

Who insulted whom by calling him a Banbury cheese?
Answer on page 144

EXPERT ADVICE

How to tell when your roast is done
Insert a metal skewer into the thickest part of the joint. Leave the skewer in place for 10 seconds, then draw it out and place it on the inside of your wrist.
• If the skewer is cool or barely warm, the meat is uncooked.
• If the skewer is very warm but bearable on your skin, the meat is cooked rare.
• If the skewer is too hot to rest on your skin for more than a second, the meat is well done.
Alternatively, you can just use a meat thermometer: 60°C for medium pink, 80°C for well-done.

GOOD ENOUGH TO EAT

Francis Bacon, painter (1909–1992)
Kevin Bacon, actor (1958–)
Chet Baker, US jazz trumpet player (1929–88)
Dame Janet Baker, opera singer (1933–)
Josephine Baker, French entertainer (1906–75)
Halle Berry, actor (1966–)
Jonathan Cake, actor (1967–)
Jasper Carrot, comedian (1945–)
Hamilton Fish, US politician (1808–93)
Elizabeth Fry, prison reformer (1780–1845)
Lady Caroline Lamb, writer and Byron's lover
(1785–1828)
Charles Lamb, essayist and poet (1775–1835)
Jack Lemmon, actor (1925–2001)
Meatloaf, singer (1947–)
Jelly Roll Morton, jazz player (1890–1941)
Captain Lawrence Edward Grace Oates, explorer
(1880–1912)
Sir Peter Neville Luard Pears, British tenor (1910–1986)
Alan Sugar, founder of Amstrad (1947–)

A SPOT OF DINNER

The most expensive meal per head was enjoyed by six diners at Petrus in London in July 2001. The bill came to £44,007, which didn't include the cost of the meal itself, which the management happily wiped from the bill. The five-figure total was for the drinks alone, which were as follows: a bottle of Chateau Petrus vintage claret at £12,300; a bottle of Chateau Petrus 1945 at £11,600; a bottle of Chateau Petrus 1946 at £9,400; a bottle of Chateau d'Yquem dessert wine at £9,200; and a bottle of Montrachet 1982 at £1,400. The remaining few pounds and pennies paid for water, fruit juice and champagne.

STRANGE DIETS

A Dutchman who has eaten pigeon food for three meals a day for the last 11 years claims it could be the answer to world famine.

Gerben Hoeksma, 58, from Veendam, says his meals are nutritious, filling and cost him next to nothing. He told *Dagblad van het Noorden*: 'I let the food soak in water for a night and then cook it the next day to get it softer.'

'It has all the substances a man needs daily. Maybe it would be good food for the people in Africa. Since I started to eat pigeon food I never felt so good. I've never been sick in my life.'

FOOD FOR THOUGHT

Ten things that are banned in organic food

Aspartame – artificial sweetener that can cause dizziness, nausea, headaches and diarrhoea

Genetic modification – can cause allergic reactions

Herbicides – destroy the life of the soil and reduce plant and wildlife species

Hydrogenated fat – linked to heart disease

Monosodium glutamate – can cause dizziness, headaches and asthma attacks

Phosphoric acid – linked to osteoporosis

Sulphur dioxide – can cause problems for asthmatics

Hormones – the level of artificial hormones in food and water can upset our individual hormone levels

Artificial colourings – have been linked to allergies and hyperactivity in children

Artificial flavourings – why would you need them?

THE DEEPER MEANING OF FOOD

In *The Meaning of Liff* and *The Deeper Meaning of Liff*, Douglas Adams and John Lloyd addressed the troubling problem that there are many everyday events in life for which there is no recognised word. And yet, there are plenty of place names hanging about the countryside that seemed to describe them perfectly. So the two were brought together, and the result is pure absurdist joy.

Abinger (n.) One who washes up everything except the frying-pan, the cheese-grater and the saucepan which the chocolate sauce has been made in.

Aigburth (n.) Any piece of readily identifiable anatomy found among cooked meat.

Beccles (n.) The small bone buttons placed in bacon sandwiches by unemployed guerrilla dentists.

Berkhamsted (n.) The massive three-course mid morning blowout enjoyed by a dieter who has already done his or her slimming duty by having one teaspoonful of cottage cheese for breakfast.

Cannock chase (n.) In any box of After Eight Mints, there is always a large number of empty envelopes and no more than four or five actual mints. The cannock chase is the process by which, no matter which part of the box you insert your fingers into, or how often, you will always extract most of the empty sachets before pinning down an actual mint, or 'cannock'.

Chimbote (n.) A newly fashionable ethnic stew, which however much everyone raves about it, seems to you to have rather a lot of fish-heads in it.

Cloates point (n.) The precise instant at which scrambled eggs are ready.

Cong (n.) Strange-shaped metal utensil found at the back of the saucepan cupboard. Many authorities believe that congs provide conclusive proof of the existence of a now-extinct form of a yellow vegetable which the Victorians used to boil mercilessly.

Corstorphine (n.) A very short premptory service held in monasteries prior to teatime to offer thanks for the benediction of digestive biscuits.

Cresbard (n.) The light working lunch that Anne Hathaway used to prepare for her husband.

Cromarty (n.) The brittle sludge which clings to the top of ketchup bottles in nasty cafes.

Darenth (n.) Measure = 0.0000176mg. Defined as that amount of margarine capable of covering one hundred slices of bread to the depth of one molecule. This is the legal maximum allowed in sandwich bars in Greater London.

Eriboll (n.) A brown bubble of cheese containing gaseous matter which grows on Welsh Rarebit.

Fraddam (n.) The small awkward-shaped piece of cheese which remains after grating a large regular-shaped piece of cheese, and which enables you to grate your fingers.

Goosnargh (n.) Something left over from preparing or eating a meal, which you store in the fridge, despite knowing full well that you will never ever use it.

Gruids (n.) The only bits of an animal left after even the people who make sausage rolls have been at it.

Naples (pl.n.) The tiny depression in a piece of Ryvita.

Peoria (n.) The fear of peeling too many potatoes.

Pott Shrigley (n.) The dried remains of a week-old casserole, eaten when extremely drunk at 2am.

Throcking (v.) The action of continually pushing down the lever on a pop-up toaster in the hope that you will thereby get it to understand that you want it to toast something.

RECORD BREAKERS

Simon Sang Koon Sung (Singapore) made 8,192 noodle strings from a single piece of dough in 59.29 seconds at a rate of over 138 per second. The record was set at the Singapore Food Festival on 31 July 1994.

OLD PICTURE, NEW CAPTION

That oyster ragout is the business, thought George, as Isabel's inhibitions melted like warm butter on a plate of asparagus

KING ALFRED'S CAKES

So did Alfred the Great really burn any cakes? The story goes that while retreating from a Viking attack, the King of Wessex took refuge in the swamps of Athelney (a small area in Somerset). There he was given shelter by a peasant woman who, not knowing who he was, asked him to keep an eye on some cakes. His mind no doubt on other things, he allowed the cakes to burn and was ticked off by the aggrieved cook. However, historians agree that this is most likely apocryphal. In reality, Alfred did flee from battle into the Somerset swamps in 878, but swiftly raised an army that defeated a Danish force on the borders of Wiltshire and Somerset and earned England a temporary respite from Viking invasions. King Alfred's Cakes is also the name for a kind of fungi that grows on dead trees and looks like burnt cakes.

FIVE FATAL MEALS

In 1985, *The Lancet* reported the case of a 23-year-old model who died after eating 1lb liver, 2lbs kidney, 0.5lb steak, 1lb cheese, two eggs, two slices of bread, one cauliflower, 10 peaches, four pears, two apples, four bananas, 2lbs each of plums, carrots and grapes and two glasses of milk.

Alexander the Great died aged 32 after a prolonged bout of eating and drinking.

The day Abensee death camp was liberated, the liberating soldiers took pity on the starving prisoners and fed them pork and beans. Tragically the survivors' bodies couldn't handle the solid food, and many died while eating their first meal of freedom.

Mama Cass of fab Sixties group the Mamas and the Papas died eating a ham sandwich, though it was a heart attack, not the sandwich, that killed her.

Charles Morris Mount, who designed the McDonald's in New York's Times Square, died aged 60 at his home in Mattituck, New York in December 2002. He had a heart attack while eating breakfast. The newspaper reports did not record what he was eating.

A FINE MESS

It was for a mess of pottage – a dish of soupy food – that Esau sold his birthright to Jacob, and now the phrase stands for a cheap price paid for something worthwhile. As this suggests, 'mess' originally meant a serving of food, or a course of a meal. It also meant a group of four people sitting down to dine together, which gave rise to the military 'mess', where meals are eaten by the armed forces.

LUCKY FOOD

A few British superstitions

Hot cross buns
The cross in a hot cross bun signifies the Crucifixion. As this took place on Good Friday, it is considered lucky to eat at least one of these buns on Good Friday. Also, it is said that if you hang one in your home, the building will be protected from bad luck or fire.

Blackberries
It is considered unlucky to pick blackberries after 29 September as the Devil is supposedly in them. However, this is probably because the blackberrying season is mostly over by then, and the only remaining blackberries would not be at their best.

Nuts
If you put two nuts into the fire side by side, and give them names – yours and your true love's – it is a good sign if they glow and burn together, but if one or both burst, it means bad luck. A couple can also place two nuts in the fire to see if they will have a long and happy life together.

Apples
When bobbing for apples, the bigger the apple you seize, the greater fortune it will bring you.

Parsley
In folklore, parsley is a highly dangerous plant; one should never plant it, only allow it to seed itself. One old wives' tale even suggests that only the wicked can grow it. It is unlucky to give parsley or transplant it, as transplanting it foretells a death in the family. And if you eat parsley when pregnant, it was said to cause a miscarriage, or prevent conception in the first place. But other superstitions suggest that if a young woman sows parsley-seed she will have a child.

CHOCOLATE HISTORY

How old is your favourite bar of chocolate?

	Date first sold in the UK
Fry's Chocolate Cream	1866
Cadbury's Dairy Milk	1905
Cadbury's Bournville	1908
Cadbury's Milk Tray	1915
Cadbury's Flake	1920
Terry's Neapolitan	1922
Terry's 1767 Bitter Bar	1923
Cadbury's Creme Egg	1923
Fry's Turkish Delight	1924
Cadbury's Fruit & Nut	1928
Cadbury's Crunchie	1929
Maya Gold Fairtrade organic chocolate	1994

WHO PUT THE HONEY IN HONEYMOON?

The origin of the word honeymoon has several explanations. The OED lists 'honey-month' used in 1564 to refer to the first month after marriage, and 'honey-moon', used in 1696, to denote the same. This is thought to arise from the custom for a newly married couple to drink a potion containing honey every day for the first month of their marriage. A similar explanation is that in Saxon times newlyweds would eat honey every day, as it was thought not only to promote fertility but also to provide the necessary desire and stamina to start a family. A less happy explanation suggests that it refers to the waning of the affection of newlyweds after one month, just as the moon wanes after a month. Current usage backs this up – we tend to refer to the early trouble-free days in any venture (a new business, a new government) as 'the honeymoon period' – when optimism rules and all mistakes are lovingly forgiven before reality sets in.

WHO EATS THE MOST?

Food	Country consuming greatest amount	Position of UK in top 10
Baked beans	Ireland	2nd
Canned food	Sweden	2nd
Chewing gum	Andorra	Not in top 10
Chocolate	Switzerland	4th
Coffee	Finland	Not in top 10
Crisps	UK	1st
Frozen food	Denmark	5th
Ice cream	Australia	Not in top 10
Meat	US	Not in top 10
Soft drinks, fizzy	US	9th
Sugar	Macedonia	Not in top 10
Tea	Ireland	4th

THE TRUTH ABOUT JACK HORNER

Little Jack Horner
Sat in a corner,
Eating a Christmas pie;
He put in his thumb, and pulled out a plum,
And said, 'What a good boy am I!'

This nursery rhyme was said to refer to Jack Horner who was steward to the last abbot of Glastonbury, Abbot Whiting. During the dissolution of the monasteries, Abbot Whiting sent Horner to see Henry VIII with a large pie as a Christmas present. When the King examined his present, he found that it contained the deeds of 12 Somerset manors, intended as a bribe to the King to spare the monastery. The plum that Jack pulled out is thought to refer to the deeds to the Manor of Mells, which Horner kept for himself. His ancestors dispute the story, but a Thomas Horner did reside at Mells soon after the monasteries were dissolved.

FOOD FIGHTS

The largest ever recorded custard-pie fight took place on 11 April, 2000, at the Millennium Dome in London, when 3,312 custard pies were thrown in three minutes by 20 people.

GOOD FOOD FACTS

Fruit is one of nature's best medicines, and provides a tasty solution to lots of little problems. The traditional remedies here make use of the fact that many fruits are anti-bacterial and anti-viral, high in antioxidant vitamins (especially if they're organic) and rich in soluble fibre. Any **citrus fruits** will help speed the end of a **cold**, thanks to their anti-bacterial properties and high levels of vitamin C; **blackcurrants** are very good too. To soothe **coughs** and **colds**, drink **lemon** or **lime** juice mixed with hot water and honey. For **sore throats**, gargle with **lemon** juice mixed half and half with hot water, or sip homemade hot **blackcurrant** juice, made with blackcurrants, hot water and honey. For **diarrhoea**, eat **apples** or **pears, blackberries, raspberries** or **blackcurrants** – but eat in moderation or you'll make the situation worse. For **constipation**, an apple **grated** and left to go brown, then mixed with a little honey, is very effective. This is also an excellent remedy for an **upset stomach**, especially if you've been sick. Dried **apricots** and **peaches**, soaked in a little hot water will also help **constipation**, as will **melons, gooseberries** and **stewed rhubarb** (and plenty of **water**). For **cystitis** or urinary infections, eat raw **blueberries** or drink a glass of **cranberry juice** every day – both are powerfully anti-bacterial. For pus-filled **spots** or **cold sores**, apply neat **lime** or **lemon** juice with a cotton bud, as long as the skin is unbroken.

COOKING CONUNDRUMS

What does an anthropophagist eat?
Answer on page 144

SWEENEY TODD

Sweeney Todd was an apocryphal serial killer, a barber who used his barbershop as a way of finding victims. He fashioned a trapdoor under his barber's chair to quickly dispose of the bodies into the cellar. He had been killing for quite a while before he met the widow Mrs Lovett who became his lover and he began to supply her with meat for her pies. The barber's cellar was linked to the cellar and bakery of the pie shop through the catacombs of St Dunstan's Church where Sweeney Todd would dispose of any parts of the body not suitable for pies. The pair were discovered when churchgoers complained of a putrid smell and the bodies and the subterranean route between pie shop and barber shop was discovered.

Mrs Lovett, after admitting the whole story, escaped the hangman by taking poison in prison. Sweeney Todd was on trial for just one murder, as, despite the bodies being found, it was almost impossible to prove his involvement in their deaths in the age before forensic evidence. However, a conviction for one murder would be enough to send Todd to the gallows.

The story – an amalgam of fact, fiction and bloodthirsty exaggeration – was retold in penny novels, stage plays, films and finally in a musical written by Stephen Sondheim, subtitled the *Demon Barber of Fleet Street*.

Sweeney Todd has since become a popular name for barbers everywhere – and for a pie shop in Reading.

STRANGE DIETS

An Indian woman has become famous for her habit of eating huge chunks of ice every day for the last 15 years. Shanti Devi from Bhiwani in Haryana eats up to 3kg of ice every day in cold weather and up to 10kg in the summer. She started eating ice when she was advised it would relieve her severe stomach ache and has never stopped.

The woman, known locally as the 'Ice Grandma', says she cannot sleep without eating ice but has been advised by her doctor to reduce her intake because of old age. The 81-year-old told *United News of India* in 2003: 'I am taking ice daily for the last 15 years in all seasons. During hot days I consume between 8–10kgs but these days due to doctor's restriction I eat only 2–3kgs ice.'

Shanti Devi's son Badlu Ram pointed out that he found it difficult initially to arrange large quantities of ice for his mother, but neighbours had helped out by offering ice stocked in their refrigerators.

CULINARY LEGENDS

Paul Bocuse is the latest in a long family line of French chefs and restaurateurs that dates back to 1765. He began his career at the age of 16 at a restaurant in Lyon and worked under several chefs before taking over his family's failing restaurant in 1959, saving it from ruin. His trademark has been to refresh the classics of French cuisine, using simpler recipes, market-fresh food and emphasising natural flavours and textures. This lighter style caught on with many younger chefs, and Bocuse has become a tireless ambassador of French cuisine, giving lectures and masterclasses around the world. While modernising the cuisine, he has lost none of the French love of rich foods; among his creations are black truffle soup, lobster Meursault and a chocolate gâteau.

A TASTY READ

Babycakes, Armistead Maupin
The Ballad of the Sad Café, Carson McCullers
Breakfast at Tiffany's, Truman Capote
Cakes and Ale, Somerset Maugham
Christmas Pudding, Nancy Mitford
Cider with Rosie, Laurie Lee
The Cider House Rules, John Irving
A Clockwork Orange, Anthony Burgess
Dinner at the Homesick Restaurant, Anne Tyler
Eating People is Wrong, Malcolm Bradbury
The Edible Woman, Margaret Atwood
Eggs, Beans and Crumpets, PG Wodehouse
The Famished Road, Ben Okri
The Grapes of Wrath, John Steinbeck
The Ginger Man, JP Donleavy
An Ice-Cream War, William Boyd
Lamb, Bernard McLaverty
The Naked Lunch, William Burroughs
Oranges Are Not The Only Fruit, Jeanette Winterson
The Pumpkin Eater, Penelope Mortimer
Sacred Hunger, Barry Unsworth
Sour Sweet, Timothy Mo
The Sugar House, Antonia White
Whisky Galore, Compton Mackenzie

EAT YOUR GREENS

In 2002, a first-year university student, overwhelmed with excitement at the size of his student loan, spent virtually all the money on an electric guitar within days of starting his course. Too ashamed to own up to his parents, he hit on the idea of feeding himself with a catering-size pack of oatmeal. He was admitted to hospital over the Christmas holidays with malnutrition.

UNUSUAL DELICACIES

The eyes of a roasted lamb's head are considered to be delicacies offered to honoured guests in Saudi Arabia.

In most countries of the Middle East, lamb's or calf's brains are commonly sold by butchers and sought after by many a housewife.

Cock's combs (*crette de coq*) are often used by French and Italian chefs to garnish various poultry dishes. Gourmets claim that cock's combs are very tasty, if a little chewy.

In Central and South America iguana meat is sautéed, then casseroled, a dish considered to be a gastronomic delight.

Eskimos consider seal blubber and whale fat to be very tasty. Cod tongues and seal flipper pie are Newfoundland specialities, and regularly found on restaurant menus.

Australian aboriginals consider chopped marinated kangaroo tail ragout to be delicious.

For centuries, both bear paw and steak have been highly prized in China, Russia and eastern European countries. Today it is almost impossible to buy bear meat commercially, but hunters still can find recipes in old eastern European cook books.

Shark fins and birds' nests, especially those from southern Java, Indonesia, are considered to be delicacies by Chinese gourmets, particularly in Hong Kong. Both are available dried in Hong Kong, Singapore and North America, and used for delicious soups.

Live snake meat is readily available in Singapore, Hong Kong and Taiwan. Sautéed snake meat and snake soup are said to ward off common colds, and to be a healthy dish.

EXPERT ADVICE

If you're a little fuzzy on those hygiene rules, here are six tips for a safer kitchen:

• Check your fridge temperature with a thermometer. The coldest part of the fridge should measure no more than 5°C. Defrost regularly – iced-up fridges don't stay cold as easily.

• Wash hands after handling raw foods and before touching other foods and utensils. Keep raw foods separate from cooked and ready-to-eat food, particularly raw meat and fish. Don't put cooked food on a plate that has previously held raw foods. Use separate chopping boards for raw and cooked foods.

• Thaw food by placing it on the bottom shelf of the fridge in a container to catch any juices. These juices can be contaminated, so wash the dish (and your hands) after handling. Thaw food in a microwave oven only if you're going to cook it straight away.

• Never refreeze food once it has been thawed. Once it has begun to thaw, it's too late to refreeze it. This also means that if you make, for example, a chicken casserole with frozen chicken, you can't freeze the leftovers.

• Don't put hot food directly into the fridge or freezer – let it cool first, or it will heat up the entire fridge. Eat leftovers within two days.

• Never reheat foods more than once. However tempting they look.

RECORD BREAKERS

The largest pancake in the world was cooked up in Rochdale in the UK in 1994. The cooks whipped up a 15.01m pancake, 2.5cm deep, weighing three tonnes.

OLD PICTURE, NEW CAPTION

As his fiancée's Sweetbread Special crawled through his digestive system, Frobisher wondered if it was too late to call off the wedding.

DO NOT ADJUST YOUR TOASTER

In 2003, researchers at Leeds University spent three months calculating a scientific formula for the making of perfect toast. They concluded that the solution lay in achieving the correct relationship between the heat of the bread and the temperature and weight of the butter. While the mathematical formula is of no use to most of us at the breakfast table, the researchers did make some useful recommendations, including:

a) that the bread needs to reach 120°C to turn golden brown; b) that the butter should be taken from the fridge and spread on the toast within two minutes of its popping up from the toaster; c) that the butter should be one-seventeenth the thickness of the bread.

EIGHT FOODS OF LOVE

Agape – a frugal meal that early Christians took together:
from the Greek *agape*, meaning 'love'

Amourettes – spinal bone marrow of beef, veal or mutton

Baiser – a French *petit four* of two meringues joined with
cream or buttercream

Hearts of palm – the buds of certain palm trees that can
be eaten raw in a salad

Lovage – an aromatic herb with a taste similar to celery

Kissing crust – the pale, slightly underbaked part of the
crust left where one loaf touched another

Kissel – a Russian dessert made of sweetened and
thickened red fruit purée

Liaison – any mixture or ingredient used to bind or thick-
en sauces, soups or stews

Puits d'amour – a small pastry made of two rounds
of puff pastry sandwiched together with jam or
confectioner's custard

A GANNET IS JUST FOR CHRISTMAS

For a few residents of the Outer Hebrides, Christmas
dinner consists not of turkey, but of baby gannet. A local
delicacy, it can be hard to come by, but once a year, the
residents of Ness on the Isle of Lewis are allowed to cull
a small number of young gannets for their festive dinner.
The gannet, or 'guga', is eaten just with boiled potatoes,
instead of all the trimmings that the rest of us expect. The
flavour is described as being between that of a duck and
a mackerel, with an oily skin (the gannet oozes black oil
before it is cooked). To prepare a gannet, the cook must
scrape off the salt covering with which it is sold, soak it
overnight and boil it for 90 minutes, with several changes
of water, during which process it reportedly smells
absolutely terrible.

THE FOOD OLYMPICS

British Olympic Gold Medal winners with foodie names:

Applegarth, Willie ....Athletics (1912)
Bacon, Stanley...Wrestling (1908)
Berry, Arthur..Football (1908)
Butler, Guy ....Athletics (1920)
Cook, Stephanie.....................Modern Pentathlon (2000)
Cooke, Harold..Hockey (1920)
Cornet, George..Swimming (1908)
Currie, Lorne ....Yachting (1900)
Miller, Charles ....Polo (1908)
Miller, George...Polo (1908)
Pike, JF ....Shooting (1908)

THE DEVIL'S PORRIDGE

In 1915, Britain seemed in danger of losing the war through lack of munitions, until 30,000 men and women turned up for work at a factory on the Solway in a quiet corner of rural Scotland to help mix the 'Devil's Porridge'. This was a highly explosive mixture of nitro-glycerine and nitro-cotton, which was so volatile that the factory workers who 'kneaded' the porridge could not wear any loose items of jewellery or clothing in case they fell into the mixture. The paste was dried, rolled into lengths called cordite and put into shells and bullets. The sheer number of workers involved meant that the factory could turn out 1,000 tonnes of the paste every week, more than all the other plants in Britain put together. The factory had its own railway with 125 miles of track, its own power station and water treatment centre and its own bakery to feed the workers, and two new towns were built to house them. The poetic name of Devil's Porridge was coined by Sir Arthur Conan Doyle, after he visited the factory in 1918.

TAKE ONE TRUFFLE TWICE DAILY

When chocolate was first brought to Europe, physicians used it as a medicine, as it was considered to be an effective treatment for a wide range of illnesses. These included:

anaemia
consumption
emaciation
faintness of heart
gout
kidney stones
low virility
mental fatigue
physical fatigue
poor appetite
poor bowel function
poor breast milk production
poor digestion
poor kidney function
shortness of breath
sluggish nervous system

BUT IS IT ART?

In 2003, artist Dave Ball created a sculpture out of 10,500 pink wafer biscuits for an exhibition in west Wales called *The Joy of Kitsch*. His sweet work of art was an attempt to recreate Carl Andre's *Equivalent VIII*, the infamous pile of bricks bought by the Tate Gallery in 1972, which caused outrage among art critics and the general public. The manager of Carmarthen's Oriel Myrddin Gallery, where 24-year-old Ball exhibited his edible masterpiece, said that he didn't think that customers would eat the exhibit, but noted that Ball had left them a few spare biscuits, just in case.

YOU ARE WHAT YOU EAT

The connection between diet and health has been made from the earliest times, most memorably by a Greek physician called Galen, who developed his theories about diet and health in the 1st century AD. The basic theory was that human beings were made up of four 'humours' – blood, bile, phlegm and black bile – which corresponded to the four elements in nature and therefore in food – air, fire, water and earth. So if, for example, a man appeared to have an excess of bile, he would be advised to avoid hot (fire) foods and eat cool (earth) foods.

A similar system is still adhered to in China and other Asian countries, where foods are divided into yin (cool) and yang (hot). The only problem in the earliest days of this theory was that there was no basis for deciding which food corresponded to which humour, and the eventual list of foods and humours was somewhat arbitrary.

Galen's medical writings survived translation into Syriac (by the Syrians), then into Arabic (when Syria fell to the Arabs), and finally into Latin by Constantine the African, a learned traveller who settled in Salerno in Italy, where a medical school had grown up after the fall of the Roman empire. By this time, Galen's works had acquired Arabic, Persian, Chinese and Indian influences and new information, all of which formed the basis of medical knowledge for almost 1,500 years.

IT MUST HAVE BEEN SOMETHING THEY ATE

The number of reported cases of food poisoning in the UK rose from 59,721 in 1990 to 98,076 in 2000.

27 WAYS TO GET YOUR OATS

Porridge is to the Scots what snow is to the Eskimos – something that needs more than one word to describe it.

blenshaw – a drink of oatmeal, sugar, milk, water and nutmeg

brochan – thick or thin gruel; sometimes used to mean porridge

brose – a dish of oat or pease-meal mixed with boiling water or milk, with salt and butter added. You can also have **athole brose** (mixed with whisky), **hasty brose** (made quickly), **kail brose** (made with the liquid from boiled kail), **neep brose** (made with the liquid from boiled turnips), **nettle brose** (made with the juice of boiled young nettle-tops) and **water brose** (mixed with boiling water; also known as **water broo**)

cauld steer(ie) – oatmeal stirred in cold water (or sour milk)

drammlicks – the small pieces of oatmeal dough which stick to the basin when making oatcakes

forrach – buttermilk, whipped cream or whey with oatmeal stirred in

froh milk – a mixture of cream and whey beaten and sprinkled with oatmeal

girsle – a fragment of crisp or caked porridge

graddan – a coarse oatmeal made from parched grain

grits – oat kernels

lithocks – a kind of gruel made from fine oatmeal and buttermilk

meal, male – oatmeal

meal an thrammel – meal stirred up with water or ale

pap-in – a drink made of light ale and oatmeal, with a little whisky or brandy

parritch, poshie – child's word for porridge

pottage – oatmeal porridge

purry – a savoury dish of oatmeal brose with chopped kail. **Tartan purry** adds chopped red cabbage or boiled cabbage water

skink – a kind of thin, oatmeal and water gruel

snap and rattle – toasted oatcakes crumbled in milk

sowce – a messy mixture, specifically an oatmeal dish like porridge

WHAT DID YOU COOK
IN THE WAR, GRANDMA?

In World War II, ration books appeared in September 1939 and by January 1940 the first items of food were being rationed. Each person was restricted to 4oz bacon or ham and 4oz of butter per week. As the war went on the list of rationed food got longer. At its peak, in August 1942, the allowance for each person per week was:

1s 2d worth of meat (eg a pork chop and four sausages)
8oz of sugar
8oz of butter, margarine or lard
4oz of bacon or ham (eg four rashers of bacon)
2oz of tea (half a packet or the equivalent of 15 teabags)
2oz of cheese
1 egg

Jam, rice, dried fruit, canned tomatoes and peas, breakfast cereals and condensed milk, chocolate, sweets, biscuits and oat flakes were also rationed.

The unexpected result was that everyone ate better because they ate less fat, less meat and more vegetables. Also, because everyone got the same, the poor often ate as well as the rich, and better than they had before the war. Farming increased and imports decreased as people went back to the land. Nearly half the families in London had an allotment or a garden to grow their own vegetables and salads. They even grew cabbages in Kensington Gardens.

SERVICE NOT INCLUDED

The habit of tipping is said to have begun in the tea gardens of London, where locked wooden boxes were left on the tea tables, and inscribed with the letters T.I.P.S. If customers were impatient, they would drop a coin or two in the box 'to insure prompt service'.

BEFORE THEY WERE FAMOUS

Some early occupations of well-known people:

Robert Burns – farmer
Michael Caine – Billingsgate fish porter
Jimmy Carter – peanut farmer
Frank Finlay – butcher
Benny Hill – milkman
Ho Chi Minh – hotel worker and pastry cook
Bob Hoskins – market porter
Magnus Pyke – nutritionist
Jimmy Tarbuck – milkman
Tennessee Williams – waiter

CHEESE ROLLING

Every year in Gloucestershire, an 8lb Double Gloucester cheese is rolled down the steep hill at Cooper's Hill, followed at breakneck speed by up to 20 competitors hurling themselves down the hill in its wake. The first person to arrive at the foot of the hill wins the cheese, and this is a sufficient reward for competitors to risk the extremely steep and uneven slope. Minor injuries are virtually guaranteed, and yet competitors (particularly the successful ones) enter the race year after year.

It is not known exactly when the annual Gloucestershire 'Cheese Rolling and Wake' began, but there is evidence that it was already an established tradition in the early 1800s. It could have evolved from ancient fertility rites, hopes of a successful harvest or to safeguard the 'Commoners' Rights' of the inhabitants of the hill.

During the rationing period of 1941–1954 a wooden substitute was used, which had a small niche that contained a token piece of cheese. When, as occasionally happens, the race has to be cancelled, a small ceremony takes place with a single cheese rolled, to maintain the tradition.

A LAND OF PLENTY

The original meanings of a few British place names:

Accrington – Acorn Farm
Croydon – Saffron Valley
Ely – Eel
Gateshead – Goats Head
Gatwick – Goat Farm
Lundy – Puffin
Purley – Pear-tree Wood
Ramsey – Land of Wild Garlic
Rievaulx – Rye Valley
Stranraer – Fat Peninsula
Swindon – Pig Hill
Tintagel – Throat Fort

REALLY USEFUL RESEARCH

Researchers at the University of Illinois conducted a survey in 2003 to find what kind of food men and women choose to cheer themselves up. The results showed that, apart from ice cream, there is a marked difference between the sexes:

Women	Men
Ice cream	Ice cream
Anything chocolate	Pizza
Biscuits and cakes	Steaks and burgers
Crisps	Pasta
Sweets	Macaroni and cheese, mashed potatoes, green bean casserole

The conclusion that the researchers drew was that men wanted home-cooked food like mother used to make, whereas women wanted instant food that they didn't have to prepare.

IT'S THE REAL THING

Curry is a much misunderstood food. The original word, *kari*, means simply 'sauce', and refers to a sauce that was poured over rice, lentils or any other food to give it a flavour. However, it was only a relish rather than the bulk of the dish. Also, it was not mouth-burningly hot. Chillis, now an integral part of the very hot curries some people inflict on themselves in a quest for 'authenticity', did not appear in India until the 1500s, when they were introduced there from the Americas. During the era of the East India Company, the Europeans devised formulae for the spice mixtures, and in 1889, at the Universal Paris Exhibition, the composition of curry powder was fixed at 34g tamarind, 44g onion, 20g coriander, 5g chilli pepper, 3g turmeric, 2g cumin, 3g fenugreek, 2g pepper and 2g mustard. However, in India, the spices vary almost infinitely according to the region, caste, customs and the whims and preferences of the cook.

THE COST OF LIVING

We all complain about inflation, but how much has your bread and butter really gone up by?

	1952	1977	2004
White bread	6d	22p	60p
Butter lb	2/6d	54p	£1.54
Beef sirloin lb	2/6d	£1.41	£4.98
Back bacon lb	3/9d	95p	£2.82
Tea 1/4lb	11d	29p	69p (125g)
Granulated sugar 2lb ..	1/	26.5p	57p
Eggs (doz)	5/3d	53p	£1.55
Potatoes (lb)	2d	4p	45p
Apples (lb)	6d	24p	68p
Pint of beer	1/3d	26.5p	£2

COOKING CONUNDRUMS

I can sizzle like bacon,
I am made with an egg,
I have plenty of backbone, but lack a good leg,
I peel layers like onions, but still remain whole,
I can be long, like a flagpole, yet fit in a hole,
What am I?
Answer on page 144

FOOD FOR THOUGHT

World War II showed the need for Britain to have greater
self-sufficiency when it came to growing its own food. It
also encouraged the development and production of chemicals for weapons and explosives. The war over, the chem-
ical-producing companies lobbied for greater use of chemicals in agriculture, given that they had quite a lot left over.

Although farmers resisted at first, the *Agriculture Act of
1947* paid out generous subsidies on bags of fertilisers,
encouraging farmers to rely more on chemical aids. Yield
increased, but soil quality decreased, requiring more chemicals to be ploughed into the land. In the chemically fer-
tilised soil, plants became more prone to insect and fungal
attacks, and weeds grew more rapidly. These were treated
with pesticides and herbicides.

In 1974, subsidies on fertilisers were dropped, but crops
themselves were subsidised, meaning that farmers received
a guaranteed price regardless of demand. Too much food
was produced, so much of the surplus was exported to
developing countries, undercutting the local farmers.
Many of them went out of business and moved to urban
centres in search of work, where Western aid in the form
of cheap bread and milk helped them to survive. Today,
some food surpluses are still sold overseas where they are
not needed.

STRANGE DIETS

Hira Ratan Manek, a retired engineer from Calicut in Kerala, claims to be able to live without solid food. He regularly embarks on long fasts, and says he has conquered hunger by absorbing solar energy through his eyes. He believes people can induce changes in their bodies by gazing at the sun every day during the first hour of sunrise or last hour of sunset while standing barefoot on the ground.

He said: 'After a few days of practice, you will feel the energy entering the body through the eyes. By receiving the sun rays through the eyes, the brain gets charged and brings out its unutilised powers.'

On 1 January 2000, Manek, who was then 65 years old, began his longest fast to date, which lasted 411 days. He drank boiled water between 11am and 4pm but consumed no other liquids or solids. He was kept under strict observation by an array of doctors and specialists, who reported that he remained in surprisingly good health. He lost 19kg in weight, but the weight loss did stabilise. The supervising doctors reported that his pulse and respiration rate slowed, but his brain function and mental capacity were unaffected.

Mr Manek said: 'Solar energy absorbed through the eyes eliminates mental illness, physical illness, spiritual ignorance and makes life happy and peaceful. One's hunger just disappears. It also activates the dormant human brain and awakens the infinite powers in human beings.'

I'LL HAVE WHAT SHE'S HAVING

Futterneid is German for 'food envy' – the feeling you get when you wish you'd ordered what your friend ordered.

OLD PICTURE, NEW CAPTION

It was fortunate for Wilson that, after his little accident, Cook's mulligatawny soup was found to be remarkably effective as a gentleman's hair restorer.

MONKEY'S BANQUET

The annual monkey banquet takes place in Lop Buri, a small town about 50 miles from Bangkok. But this is no euphemistic feast; the guests really are monkeys. The organiser, Yonguth Kijwattananuson, says that monkeys have added character and colour to the town and are consequently honoured once a year. Gourmet chefs are drafted in to prepare a feast of vegetarian delicacies, which are duly presented to the pampered primates. The ensuing food fight and general lack of any sort of table manners is generally considered as part of the fun by the mainly Buddhist locals and curious tourists.

SAY IT WITH FOOD

Seven ways to insult someone in a foodie kind of way:

Every bean has its black – everyone has their faults, a reference to black-eyed beans

Cheese it – stop it, or clear off

You're a loose fish – a person of dissolute habits. Fish is generally derogatory – a poor fish, a queer fish, a wet fish, a cold fish…

You drive your hog to market – you snore (loudly)

You have brought your hogs to a fine market – this is fine mess you've got yourself into

He's hog-shearing – he's making much ado about nothing

He's gone hog-wild – he's gone crazy

PLAYING WITH YOUR FOOD

Every year since 1999, the Yorkshire town of Brawby has held a Yorkshire Pudding race, for which participants must create a boat out of the ingredients of this tradition-al dish. Each boat requires around 50 eggs, four bags of flour and 25 pints of milk. The mixture is baked, lined with industrial foam-filler and made water-resistant with layers of yacht varnish.

The race was dreamed up by Simon Thackray, a local artist, who, while staring out of the window of his local pub one afternoon, mused: 'Wouldn't it be great to sail down a river in a giant Yorkshire pudding?' He created a small prototype from a shop-bought pudding, powered by a small electric motor, which had its maiden voyage in his bath. Despite the name, it is not so much a race as a display of creative endeavour and eccentricity. 'There is,' says Thackray, 'a start but no finish.'

COOKING CONUNDRUMS

Why is gooseberry fool called a fool?
Answer on page 144

SPUD TROUBLE

The humble potato has caused a lot of bother
throughout history...

- The Swiss believed potatoes caused scrofula.
- In 1774, the citizens of Kolberg refused to eat potatoes sent by Frederick the Great of Prussia to relieve their famine, until forced to do so by the militia.
- Until 1780, potatoes were excluded from prudent French tables, as they were thought to cause leprosy.
- Devout Scotch Presbyterians refused to eat them as they weren't mentioned in the Bible.
- In Prussia, King Frederick William I threatened to cut off the noses and ears of peasants who refused to plant them.
- Russian peasants considered them unclean and un-Christian, calling them 'Devil's apples'.

- In colonial Massachusetts, they were considered the spoor of witches.
- Ireland made the potato the foundation of its national diet; an act that was to have terrible repercussions in 1845 when a late blight attacked the potato crop and caused a devastating famine in which over a million people died.
- In 2001, Indian vegetarian lawyer Harish Bharti attempted to sue McDonald's, the omnipresent burger chain. Bharti claimed that McDonald's had misled its customers by announcing in 1990 that its fries would be cooked in 100% vegetable oil, but omitting to mention that they later added beef flavouring.

OLD PICTURE, NEW CAPTION

When Cook was trying out a new recipe, Albert couldn't always bring himself to look into the tureen.

COOKING SAINT

St Martha, who died around 80 AD, was the patron saint of cooking and the sister of the much more famous Mary Magdalene. Martha and Mary lived with their brother Lazarus in Bethany, a small town near Jerusalem. Jesus preached in Judea and often visited their home, and Martha went to great lengths to make Jesus comfortable.

As well as being the patron saint of cooks, she also watches over butlers, dieticians, domestic servants, homemakers, hotel-keepers, housemaids, housewives, innkeepers, laundry workers, maids and servants. In art, Martha is portrayed as a housewife and is often depicted with symbols of housework, such as a broom, ladle or a set of keys. Her feast day is 29th July.

SOMEONE TO WATCH OVER YOU

There are patron saints for everything, it seems,
and food is no exception:

Adrian of Nicomedia – butchers
Anthony of Padua – against starvation
Pascal Baylon – cooks,
especially New Mexican cooking
Charles Borromeo – apple orchards
Bridgid of Ireland – dairy workers
Drogo – coffee house owners
Erasmus – against abdominal pain
Elizabeth of Hungary – bakers
Honoratus – bakers, cake makers
Honorius of Amiens – confectioners
Joseph – confectioners
Lawrence – butchers, confectioners, cooks,
restaurateurs, brewers and wine makers
Macarius the Younger – pastry cooks
Martha – cooks
Michael – grocery stores
Nicholas of Myra – bakers
Urban – wine
Walburga – against famine

HONEY TROUBLE

Lovers of honey have long been troubled by the phenom-
enon that if you spread honey onto a piece of unbuttered
toast, the toast becomes concave. The reason is simple.
Bread is approximately 40% water, while honey is a con-
centrated solution made up of around 80% sugars.
Osmosis draws water out of the bread and into the
honey, causing the bread to become concave. Fortunately
the solution is also simple – a thin layer of butter or margarine will protect the toast from this distressing effect.

FAVOURITE SOUPS

Alexander II
(1855–1881, Russian tsar)
Borscht; which he would
only eat on Saxony
porcelain

Madame du Barry
(1743–1793, Louis XV's
mistress)
Cauliflower soup: she and
the King refused anything
else as a starter

Sarah Bernhardt
(1844–1923)
Bouillabaisse, which had
to be stirred with a red-hot
poker

Napoleon Bonaparte
(1769–1821) Chestnut
soup; a comfort soup after
recovering from a stomach
ache in Egypt

Eva Braun
(1910–1945, Hitler's
mistress and, very
briefly, wife)
Turtle soup

Al Capone
(1899–1947)
Minestrone – except in
1923 when arch rivals, the
Aiellos, offered the chef at
Joe Esposito's Bella Napoli

Café US$35,000
(GB£18,900) if he'd lace
the soup with prussic acid.
The chef accepted then
thought better of it and
told his good customer
about the plot.

Catherine the Great
(1762–1796)
Borscht, which she ate
from handmade silver
plates given to her by
Ukrainian Cossacks

Charles Darwin
(1809–1882)
Young tortoise soup,
which he described as
an 'excellent soup' from
his days in the Galapagos
Islands

Charles de Gaulle
(1890–1970)
Toutes les soupes –
so much so that he insisted
on a different one each day

Alexandre Dumas
(1802–1870)
Cabbage soup

Erik XIV
(16th-century
Swedish King)
Yellow pea soup – at least

until 1577 when he died
after eating a poisoned
bowlful

James A Garfield
(1831–1881, US
President)
Squirrel soup

Howard Hughes
(1905–1976)
Tinned soup, which was
all he ate after withdrawing
from the world

Vladimir Lenin
(1870–1924)
Shchi (a humble cabbage
soup he prepared himself)

Abraham Lincoln
(1809–1865, US President)
Mock turtle soup – the
soup he ordered on the
4th March 1861 at a
luncheon to celebrate his
inauguration as President

Louis XIV
(1638–1715)
Spiced broth – he was
known to eat four bowls
at both lunch and dinner.

Richard Nixon
(1913–94)
After his first state dinner
as President, Nixon com-
plained that the meal had
gone on too long and that

the soup course should
henceforth be omitted.
'Men don't really like
soup,' he explained.

Rudolf Nureyev
(1938–1992)
Borscht – according to
The Ballet Cookbook,
1966, Nureyev liked his
food to be 'a soup using
half a cow'.

Madame de Pompadour
(1721–1764, mistress to
King Louis XIV)
Celery soup, which she
thought would remedy
her sexual frigidity

Queen Victoria
(1819–1901)
Chicken and ham soup
with cream, mushrooms
and tapioca

Boris Yeltsin
(1931–2007)
Fish soup. At a working
dinner in 1995 with then
Prime Minister John Major
Yeltsin pushed away his
plate of shrimp to com-
plain: 'The prime minister
has soup and I don't.' He
was unaware that Major
had requested an alterna-
tive because shellfish do
not agree with him.

SAY IT WITH FOOD

*Pigs are a popular subject when it comes to
cautionary phrases...*

A pig's whisper – very short space of time
Bartholomew pig – a fat person; from the chief
attraction of a roasted pig at Bartholomew Fair
Like a pig in a poke – a blind bargain
Pigs in clover – people with newly acquired money
who don't know how to behave now they have it
Pig-headed – stubborn and stupid
Squealing like a stuck pig – shouting with pain
Staring like a stuck pig – with mouth open and eyes wide
To baste your bacon – to strike or scourge, as the bacon
was the outside of the pig, so would receive any blows
aimed at the unfortunate animal
To bring home the bacon – to earn the family's living,
possibly a reference to the sport of catching a greased
pig at country fairs
To eat Dunmow bacon – to live in conjugal bliss
To go to pigs and whistles – to be ruined
To make a pig's ear – to mess something up
To make a silk purse out of a sow's ear – to turn
something unpromising into a triumph
To pull bacon – to cock a snook
To save one's bacon – to rescue oneself; possibly referring
to saving the last of the bacon from the scavenging dogs
of the house
When pigs fly – never

TREMENDOUS TOFFEE

The largest piece of toffee ever made weighed 1,335.5kg
(2,940lb) and was made by Susie's South Forty
Confections Ltd in the USA in 2001 in the shape of the
state of Texas. It contained a total of 7,056,000 calories.

LOST IN TRANSLATION

The following linguistic disasters have been found on menus all over the world, as chefs attempt to translate their culinary delights into English:

Boiled frogfish – Europe
Buttered saucepans and fried hormones – Japan
Cock in wine/Lioness cutlet – Cairo
Dreaded veal cutlet with potatoes in cream – China
French creeps – LA
French fried ships – Cairo
Fried fishermen — Japan
Fried friendship – Nepal
Garlic coffee – Europe
Goose barnacles – Spain
Muscles of marines/lobster thermos – Cairo
Pork with fresh garbage – Vietnam
Prawn cock and tail – Cairo
Roasted duck let loose – Poland
Sole bonne femme (Fish landlady style) – Europe
Strawberry crap – Japan
Sweat from the trolley – Europe
Teppan yaki, before your cooked right eyes – Japan
Toes with butter and jam – Bali

SQUARE MEAL

British war ships in the 1700s did not have the best of living conditions, and when ships were away from shore for long periods of time, meals suffered. A sailor's breakfast and lunch were sparse meals consisting of little more than bread and a beverage. But the third meal of the day included meat and was served on a square tray (eating a substantial meal onboard a ship required a tray to carry it all). Hence a 'square meal' was the most substantial meal served.

FOOD FOR THOUGHT

For every dollar that the World Health Organisation spends on trying to improve the diets of people across the globe, approximately US$500 is spent by the food industry worldwide on promoting processed foods.

SEVEN SAUSAGE FACTS

- The word sausage is derived from the Latin word *salsus*, which means something salted
- Dick Turpin worked as a butcher
- Sausages are eaten at 71% of all UK barbecues
- Queen Victoria liked sausages but insisted that the meat in them be hand-chopped rather than minced
- Sausages were called bangers during World War II because they exploded when fried, due to the high water content
- Ninety per cent of British households buy sausages and 50% buy them at least once a month
- Sausages are mentioned in Homer's Odyssey:
These goat sausages sizzling here in the fire –
We packed them with fat and blood to have for supper.
Now, whoever wins this bout and proves the stronger,
Let that man step up and take his pick of the lot!

A ONE-MAN SHOW

Dave Walia set a world record when he prepared and cooked a meal single-handedly for 1,081 guests in 50 hours 30 minutes at Fissul in Portugal in October 1998. Beginning work at 10am on the 22nd, he prepared 2kg of chillies, 10kg of garlic, 10kg of ginger, and 200kg of onions. The next day he made 40 litres of yoghurt, diced 250kg of chicken breasts and on the 24th, he prepared the rice and cooked 2,000 poppadoms.

Bees could be among the most important contributors to a healthy diet. Honey, royal jelly, propolis and bee pollen are all thought to have beneficial effects. And when you learn what is in them, it is not surprising.

Honey is rich in vitamins B, C and calcium. It is a natural form of sugar, which has been proven to improve athletic performance, to help reduce insomnia and to speed the healing of wounds. Studies in New Zealand found that manuka honey taken for a month could eliminate *Helicobacter pylori* from the stomach, a major cause of stomach ulcers, and did so more efficiently than conventional drugs. It is also thought that if hay fever sufferers eat locally produced honey, it helps build their resistance to allergies caused by local pollen. Russian hospitals use honey to help heal burns, and honey has been used to heal varicose leg ulcers. Finally, studies in the UK are finding that honey has powerful anti-bacterial properties and may help in the fight against MRSA.

Royal jelly is the food of the Queen bee, secreted by nurse bees to give the queen a lifespan of up to three years. It is rich in vitamin B, enzymes, hormones and amino acids. The National Institute of Medical Herbalists say that it is well-known for its antiviral properties.

Bee pollen is rich in most B vitamins and folic acid and is believed by some to help promote fertility and conception.

Propolis contains every vitamin except K and every mineral we need apart from sulphur. It is a resinous substance collected by bees from plant buds. Russian hospitals prescribe it to aid recovery after surgery.

Needless to say, the purer and fresher the honey, the better.

EXPERT ADVICE

• To get more juice out of a lemon or lime, either bash and roll it on the worktop before cutting and squeezing it, or microwave it for 10-15 seconds before juicing.
• If you're short of space and saucepans (and stamina) at a dinner party, make the sauce ahead of time and keep it hot in a Thermos flask.
• To stop okra going slimy, sharpen the stem end to a point, like a pencil, before you cook it.
• If your pastry's a bit sticky or fragile, roll it out between two sheets of floured baking parchment.

THE REAL MR BEAN

Henry John Heinz was born in Pittsburgh in 1844 to German immigrant parents and began his retail career by selling jars of horseradish. In 1876, he and his brother John and cousin Frederick set up F&J Heinz. Their first product was ketchup, a homemade staple of every US household, but one that required a day of attentive stirring.

The business grew quickly, and by 1886 Henry was in the UK, selling his products to Fortnum and Mason. Heinz opened a company in Britain in 1905, and his beans in tomato ketchup were first made here in 1925, closely followed by tins of spaghetti, which confused a generation or two about the true consistency of pasta. Heinz fame spread all over the world, and Heinz products were even taken to the South Pole by Scott in 1910. The much-maligned Heinz Salad Cream was invented in the UK in the 1940s to liven up the wartime diet, and became so popular that plans to withdraw it in recent years raised so much protest that it was put back on sale. Today Heinz turns out 1.5 million cans of beans a day, and is the proud owner of one of the most famous advertising slogans of all time: 'Beanz Meanz Heinz'.

DOLING OUT THE RATIONS

An early form of income support was practised in Rome around 70 BC, but used food rather than money. The cost of living had risen so much that free grain was given away to the needy, about 40,000 people. The numbers rose rapidly; some years later Julius Caesar, concerned that the situation was getting out of hand, was forced to cut the number of people receiving free rations to 150,000. However the numbers went back up again and within 50 years, 320,000 people were receiving the grain – about a third of the population. Three centuries later, the problem was still not solved; the *annona* or handout consisted of bread, pork fat and wine. As the days of the Roman empire drew to a close, however, government officials were finally forced to put an end to free food distribution. The people were left to fend for themselves.

A FOODIE STORY

Thinking up a title for your memoirs is never easy, but these celebrities had their minds on food at the time...

Apple Sauce	Michael Wilding
Arias and Raspberries	Harry Secombe
Change Lobsters and Dance	Lili Palmer
Cider with Rosie	Laurie Lee
Confessions of an English Opium-Eater	Thomas de Quincey
Diet for Life	Lynn Redgrave
The Good, The Bad and The Bubbly	George Best
Grain of Wheat	Lord Longford
Let the Chips Fall	Rudy Vallee
Life is a Banquet	Rosalind Russell
The Long Banana Skin	Michael Bentine
Toast: The Story of a Boy's Hunger	Nigel Slater

FAMOUS COOKS

Peter Cook – writer, actor, comedian and the founder of *Private Eye*. Genius or madman, depending on your sense of humour.

Captain James Cook – 18th century navigator and explorer and the author of three books about his voyages to the Pacific Ocean, during which the main shorelines were discovered.

Thomas Cook – born in Derbyshire, the future travel agent started life as a Baptist missionary. He became involved in the travel business after an excursion to Loughborough for a temperance meeting led to Cook arranging the first public train excursion. He soon branched out into European train trips to become the huge international travel agent that it is today.

Alistair Cooke – journalist and broadcaster. He was famous for his *Letter from America*, which was broadcast by the BBC from 1946 until 2004. This made his radio programme the longest-running solo radio feature programme.

Robin Cook – a Labour Party politician who resigned his position as Leader of the House of Commons and Lord President of the Council in March 2003 over the British government's involvement in the conflict with Iraq. He had been foreign secretary from 1997 to 2001.

Beryl Cook – British artist who paints distinctively overweight and jovial characters. Her work is suggestive of saucy postcard humour and has been widely used on greeting cards.

Sam Cook – a famous soul singer of the 1960s who was was involved in the civil rights movement in the US. He was murdered in 1964 by an LA hotel manager.

NO FOOD, IT'S FRIDAY

The tradition of fasting was first recorded around the 2nd century, and was usually practised as a way of martyring oneself when persecuted. It evolved into a sign of holiness (and of self-control, important given what happened in the Garden of Eden), and was one way to achieve perfection and purity. At first the practice was voluntary, but by the 6th century the Church had made it compulsory. Wednesdays and Fridays were fast days, and one was expected to fast before baptism and during any period of penance. The Easter fast of Lent, originally four days long, gradually stretched into 40 days. However for most people, fasting meant abstaining from certain foods rather than eating nothing at all. Still, when fast days came to include every Wednesday, Friday and Sunday as well as Lent, even that became a bit trying. The ordinary man, if he dared, could risk a little discreet cheating, but it was no small risk – until the mid-1500s, it was technically possible to be hanged for eating meat on a Friday. The rules were occasionally relaxed as the Church went through phases of allowing dairy foods, eggs and fish during fasts, making Lent the most prosperous time of year for the salted fish merchants. But sooner or later there would be a fit of piety and everyone would be back on bread and vegetables.

ONE POTATO, TWO POTATO

If potato varieties to you means mashed, boiled or baked, read on – England has literally hundreds potato varieties to taste. And variety, as they say, is the spud of life:

Belle de Fontanay • Charlotte • Desiree • Duke of York
Dundrod • Estima • Fianna • Golden Wonder • Kerr's
Pink • Linzer Delikates • Marfona • Lady Balfour
Nadine • Pentland • Javelin • Pink Fir Apple
Premiere • Romano • Saxon • Wilja

FEAST OF FOOLS

The Feast of Fools was a celebration that was thoroughly if rudely enjoyed in the Middle Ages. It was held on the feasts of St Stephen, St John and the Holy Innocents which, conveniently, were on the 26th, 27th and 28th December. Although it centred on a cathedral, the purpose was to mock and disrupt the ceremony, and to indulge in obscene jests and dancing. It was eventually suppressed during the Reformation.

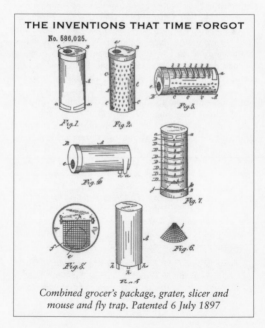

THE INVENTIONS THAT TIME FORGOT
No. 586,025.

Combined grocer's package, grater, slicer and mouse and fly trap. Patented 6 July 1897

BULKING UP

In the 19th century, as the population grew and the food industry had to keep pace, unscrupulous manufacturers and traders took to bulking up or enhancing their product with other less expensive ingredients:

Boiled sweets were coloured with salts of copper and lead (poisonous)

Bread was often (unsafely) whitened with alum

China tea was mixed with thorn leaves coloured with verdigris (poisonous)

Coffee was diluted with ground chicory or acorns

Cocoa was diluted with brick dust

Gloucester cheese owed its red rind to a red lead colouring (poisonous)

Pepper was bulked out with mustard husks, pea flour and dust swept up from the floor

Pickles were made green with copper (poisonous)

Tea leaves were often mixed with dried ash leaves; merchants also took used tea leaves, dried them, coloured them black with lead (poisonous) and resold them

Wine was flavoured with bitter almonds, containing prussic acid (poisonous)

SALAD DAYS

Shakespeare first used the phrase 'salad days' in *Antony and Cleopatra, Act 1, Scene 5*. When Cleopatra lavishes praise on her new love, Antony, one of her attendants reminds the queen that she once felt the same for Caesar. Cleopatra replies that she was in her 'salad days, when I was green in judgment: cold in blood'. Cleopatra meant it to mean youthfully naïve, but it has come to mean the best days of one's youth, when life is still full of unexplored potential. It was later the title of a 1950s musical.

WHAT'S FOR PUDDING?

Black pudding is a delicacy all over Europe, and like
many gourmet delicacies, it has countless regional and
national variations. Here are a few things that are added
to the key ingredient of pig's blood:

Alsace, France – pork rind and fat, ears, head,
trotters and onions
Auvergne, France – milk and crackling; chestnuts
Brittany, France – prunes
Brussels, Belgium – eggs, butter and cream
Flanders – raisins
Lyon, France – raw onions marinated in brandy and herbs
Nancy, France – milk
Normandy, France – apples
Paris, France – cooked onions
Poitou, France – cooked spinach, cream, semolina and eggs
Kerry, Ireland – sheep's blood
Lecce, Italy – pig's brains
Scandinavia – raisins
Sicily – raisins, almonds, candied pumpkin
Spain – onions, rice and flavourings such as aniseed,
cloves and other spices, rice, pine nuts

CULINARY LEGENDS

Marcus Gavius Apicius, born about 25 AD, is believed to
be the author of one of the world's oldest cookbooks, *De
Re Coquinaria Libri Decem* (Cuisine in Ten Books). He
was known for his expensive tastes, and was perhaps the
original inventor of the idea of foie gras, as he devised a
way of feeding dried figs to pigs to fatten their livers.
According to the *Larousse Gastronomique*, he spent
extravagantly on numerous banquets, and when he ran out
of money, he preferred to poison himself rather than scale
back his lifestyle.

COOKING CONUNDRUMS

My first is in soup and also in spoon • My second's in
honey and also in moon • My third is in whiting but
never in sprat • My fourth is in marrow but never in fat
My fifth is in gin but never in rye • My whole is quite
complex and potent, you'll cry • What am I?
Answer on page 144

LUCKY FOOD

A few American superstitions

Before slicing a new
loaf of bread, make the
sign of the cross on it.

A loaf of bread should
never be turned upside
down after a slice has
been cut from it.

A fish should always be
eaten from the head
toward the tail.

To drop a fork means a
man is coming to visit.

If you bite your tongue
while eating, it is because
you have recently lied.

An onion cut in half and
placed under the bed of a
sick person will draw off
fever and poisons.

A wish will come true if
you make it while burning
onions.

If you spill pepper you
will have a serious argu-
ment with your best
friend.

Rosemary planted by
the doorstep will keep
witches away.

Salty soup is a sign
that the cook is in love.

If a single woman sleeps
with a piece of wedding
cake under her pillow, she
will dream of her future
husband.

It's bad luck to let milk
boil over.

57

www.carrotmuseum.com
The home of the World Carrot Museum, a virtual institution that will tell you everything you need to know about this humble vegetable.

www.cheese.com
Although this is a sales site, it does list every cheese you will ever want to eat or identify.

www.sausagelinks.com
Sausage information, sausage of the week and sausage news.

www.chocolate.org
Less about eating and more about science, this links to lots of academic research about chocolate. If you eat a lot of chocolate, this can help you to justify your habit.

www.chocophile.com
Full of mouthwatering articles and news, and updated regularly, with links to lots of good chocolatiers.

www.foodsubs.com
Identifies every ingredient you can think of, so particularly useful for exotic produce and for deciphering UK/US terms.

www.nicecupofteaand asitdown.com
Cheerfully daft and very extensive; offers more information on biscuits than you'll need, including answers to such questions as 'Is a Jaffa cake a biscuit?' and 'What's the story with pink wafers?' Log on for biscuit of the week, a survey of fig rolls and how to make underpant toast.

www.soupsong.com
Utterly wonderful, seemingly endless and the best source of soup jokes in the universe, such as US comic Steven Wright's immortal line: 'I put instant soup in the microwave and almost went back in time.'

www.tea.co.uk
Interesting and varied site run by the Tea Council, which, though largely grown-up and sensible, is frivolous enough to offer a daily tealeaf reading.

A SHORT ESSAY ON
CHRISTMAS PUDDING

What we now know as Christmas pudding was first made as a Christmas Eve dish of frumenty, a soupy dish of hulled wheat cooked in milk. In the early Middle Ages, it was made with meat broth, oatmeal, eggs, currants, dried plums and spices and was known as 'plum porridge', or 'pottage'. It was served with the first course and eaten with a spoon and was a favourite of Henry VIII. In Elizabethan times, it became thicker as they replaced the oats with breadcrumbs and added suet and ale or wine.

Oliver Cromwell banned it in 1664, disapproving of its boozy contents, calling it 'a lewd custom'. But Cromwell failed to abolish either the monarchy or Christmas pudding, and George I reinstated the dish 50 or so years later. By this time we had learned how to steam it in a pudding cloth, and it took on a perfectly round 'cannonball' shape. The Victorians took out the plums and added raisins, currants and dried peel. Finally, in the 20th century it was poured into a basin, covered with the pudding cloth and steamed, thereby taking on its most recent shape.

But the most important thing to know about Christmas pudding is how to set it alight. The secret is to gently warm the brandy in a pan, scoop some up in an heatproof ladle, set fire to the brandy, and then pour it on to the pudding.

FEEDING THE IMAGINATION

On emerging from one of his creative binges, during which he reportedly lived on too much coffee, eggs and fruit, Honoré de Balzac, author of *La Comédie Humaine*, embarked on a long feast during which he ate 100 Ostend oysters, 12 cutlets of salt-meadow mutton, a duck with turnips, two partridges and a Normandy sole, as well as desserts, fruit, coffee and liqueurs.

FROM THE MOUTHS OF BABES

Advice for Kids was a popular round-robin email, immortalising the wisdom of some Australian pre-teens. Several (not surprisingly) involved food:

Never trust a dog to watch your food – Patrick, age 10

Never tell your mom her diet's not working – Michael, age 14

Stay away from prunes – Randy, age 9

You can't hide a piece of broccoli in a glass of milk – Armir, age 9

Puppies still have bad breath even after eating tic-tacs – Andrew, age 9

Don't sneeze in front of Mom when you're eating crackers – Mitchell, age 12

TEN BAD MOMENTS IN A COOK'S LIFE

1. Seven ounces of flour left in the bag when you need eight.
2. The lingering smell of fish in the room two days after a kedgeree.
3. Not being sure whether the milk is off, and being torn between tasting it, going out to buy more or pouring it in to the ingredients and hoping for the best.
4. Lemon juice in a cut.
5. A casserole dish fractionally too small for your leg of lamb.
6. Waiting for a very large saucepan of water to boil.
7. Finding nine promising ingredients in the cupboard, but realising that in no combination will they actually make a meal.
8. Reading 'reserve the liquid' just after you've carefully strained said liquid down the sink.
9. Finding only beef stock cubes when your guests are vegetarian, and wondering how bad it would be if...
10. Smoke alarms.

SAY IT WITH FOOD

Phrases to leave you hungry...

Banyan day – a meat-free day, as recorded by the English navy; the day when their rations included no meat

Tis a Barmecide's feast – a disappointing illusion (from the Barmecide family in *Arabian Nights*)

To dine with Democritus (or with Duke Humphrey, or with the cross-legged knights) – to get no dinner

To give one a baker's dozen – to give someone a beating (the baker's dozen representing one blow too many)

I'll give him beans – I'll give him a thrashing

The big gooseberry season – silly season for the newspapers

To eat dog – to perform an unpleasant task for another. American Indians ate dogs at important meetings, a custom to which white men took exception. They were eventually allowed to offer a silver dollar for someone else to eat the dog for them

To eat one's terms – to be studying for the bar. Students have to eat in the hall of an Inn of Court at least three times in each of the 12 terms before they are called to the bar

To eat the leek – to eat one's words

To take bread and salt – to take an oath

To return to our muttons – to get back to the subject

To pepper one well – to give someone a beating, or shoot at them

To have a finger in every pie – to be involved in or have a share in; not usually meant as a compliment

EXPERT ADVICE

How to choose the ideal saucepan:

Aluminium
Pros: second most effective heat conductor; lightweight and easy to lift
Cons: easily dented; must be coated with a non-stick surface, as aluminium reacts with certain foods

Cast iron
Pros: Even heat distribution, holds high temperatures well; relatively inexpensive
Cons: Very heavy; must be kept oiled to prevent rusting

Glass
Pros: Good for watching contents of pan; attractive; useful in microwave and oven
Cons: Poor heat conductor; breaks easily

Stainless steel
Pros: Hard, durable; good for keeping food warm and for low-temperature cooking
Cons: Poor heat conductor, so needs a copper or aluminium base, or aluminium core to increase heat conductivity. If it has these, it is the best option and is much used professional kitchens

Copper
Pros: Excellent heat conductor, heats and cools rapidly and evenly
Cons: Must be lined with tin, as copper reacts with certain foods, and the tin lining must be replaced periodically; heavy, often expensive; needs frequent cleaning

Enamel
Pros: Conducts heat evenly; hard-wearing
Cons: If poorly made, the enamel can crack, leaving space for bacteria to grow; requires wooden utensils to avoid scratching the enamel

OLD PICTURE, NEW CAPTION

*'It's the Cook,' gasped Charles. 'I've told her a hundred
times not to use those damned tobasco chillis.'*

DORMOUSE PIE

Lewis Carroll may have been on to something when he
put his fictional dormouse in a teapot. This small rodent
was a delicacy in Roman times, and the Romans fattened
them up by keeping them in small dried mud containers,
and feeding them acorns and chestnuts through a small
hole. When deemed plump enough, they were stewed or
roasted and coated with honey and seeds. Dormouse pie
continued to be enjoyed in France until the 17th century.

SO THAT'S WHAT THEY
MEAN BY HIGH TABLE

The highest formal meal eaten was served at 6,768m (22,205ft) at the top of Mount Huascaran in Peru on 28 June 1989. Nine members of the Ansett Social Climbers from Sydney scaled the mountain with a Louis XIV dining table, chairs, silverware, candelabra, wine and a three-course meal.

BUG CLUB

For those whose meals lack that essential crunch, Iowa State University has an Entomology Club, which offers a batch of tasty insect recipes, available on the internet, for such delicacies as Bug Blox, Banana Worm Bread, Rootworm Beetle Dip, Chocolate Chirpie Chip Cookies, Crackers and Cheese Dip with Candied Crickets, Mealworm Fried Rice, Corn Borer Cornbread Muffins and Chocolate-covered Grasshoppers. They also helpfully provide a nutritional chart (a dung beetle contains 17.2g protein, for example, and crickets are surprisingly high in calcium) as well as links to insect cookbooks and where to buy your insects.

To celebrate their unusual culinary habits, every year the Entomology Club hosts an Insect Horror Film Festival, featuring gourmet insect tasting, live insect displays, a butterfly house, informational displays, and a classic insect movie.

OUT OF THIS WORLD

When Neil Armstrong and Edwin 'Buzz' Aldrin ate their first meal on the moon, their meal – served out of foil packs – comprised roast turkey and all the trimmings.

HOME COMFORTS

When the Duke of Wellington landed at Dover in 1814, after being away from England for six years, his first request was an unlimited supply of hot, buttered toast.

CULINARY LEGENDS

Isabella Beeton (1836–1865) is fondly thought of as a wise and grandmotherly figure, but was in fact only 25 when she published *The Book of Household Management* in 1861. She did not claim to be a trained cook, but compiled recipes and advice from many sources. In the preface she states: 'What moved me in the first instance to attempt a work like this was the discomfort and suffering which I had seen brought upon men and women by household mismanagement. I have always thought that there is no more fruitful source of family discontent than a housewife's badly cooked dinners and untidy ways.'

Having grown up in a household of 21 children, including step-siblings, this view is not surprising. Her book was not just a cookbook but a complete manual to running a home, including chapters on managing servants, basic medical advice and legal matters, running to over 1,000 pages. She had been well educated, and the text is peppered with literary references and discussions on religion, science and history as well as household matters. She no doubt benefited from having a husband who not only was a wealthy publisher but also believed that an intelligent wife was a great blessing in life. Her progressive outlook is reflected in the legal chapter, which details the rights of women separated from their husbands because of ill-treatment. Mrs Beeton's life was productive but tragically brief; she died at the age of 28, of puerperal fever.

WHO WAS FANNY ADAMS?

The origin of the phrase 'sweet Fanny Adams' – abbreviated to 'sweet FA', with unfortunate connotations – has a gruesome origin. Fanny Adams was a child who in 1867 was horribly murdered and dismembered. The Royal Navy, perhaps unmoved by her fate, began to use her name to refer to their ration of tinned mutton, which was introduced about the same time. It then meant 'something worthless', and now means 'nothing at all'.

SAY IT WITH FOOD

Five porridge proverbs:

He has supped all his porridge – he has eaten his last meal/he is dead
Keep your breath to cool your porridge – keep your opinions to yourself
Not to earn salt for one's porridge – to be a layabout
To do porridge – to do time in jail
Everything tastes of porridge – whatever our fantasies may be, the mundane facts of life remain

CHINESE YORKSHIRE PUDDING

On 25 April 1970, the city of Leeds held a competition to discover Britain's best Yorkshire pudding maker. Three English hotel chefs, a Leeds University student and a housewife were humbled by Hong Kong-born Tin Sung Chan, a Chinese chef, who won first prize.

Asked the secret of his success, Chan said 'I put in a secret ingredient. It's a Chinese herb called tai luk.' The judges didn't know what it was, but they must have liked it. *The Guardian* reported that his pudding 'rose to the height of a coronation crown and its taste, according to one judge, was superb.' Chan won a holiday in Ireland.

COOKING TERMS REDEFINED

An anonymous posting on the internet,
and a small work of genius:

Calorie – basic measure of the amount of rationalisation offered by the average individual prior to taking a second helping.

Frying pan – standard instrument of destruction for eggs, pancakes, and various vegetable matter. Remains may be removed from surface with diluted solution of sulphuric acid.

Microwave oven – space-age kitchen appliance that uses the principle of radar to locate and immediately destroy any food placed within the cooking compartment.

Oven – compact home incinerator used for disposing of bulky pieces of meat and poultry.

Preheat – to turn on the heat in an oven for a period of time before cooking a dish, so that the fingers may be burned when the food is put in, as well as when it is removed.

Porridge – thick oatmeal rarely found on breakfast tables since children were granted the right to sue their parents. The name is an amalgamation of the words 'putrid', 'horrid', and 'sludge'.

Recipe – a series of step-by-step instructions for preparing ingredients you forgot to buy, in utensils you don't own, to make a dish the dog won't eat.

Tongue – a variety of meat, rarely served because it clearly crosses the line between a cut of beef and a piece of dead cow.

Yogurt – semi-solid dairy product made from partially evaporated and fermented milk. One of only three foods that taste the same as they sound. The other two are goulash and squid.

OLD PICTURE, NEW CAPTION

After the third fly-in-the-soup joke that day, Harold finally lost his sense of humour.

READ THE LABEL

Helpful advice found on food packaging...

On a bag of Fritos: You could be a winner! No purchase necessary. Details inside.

On Swanson frozen dinners: Serving suggestion: Defrost.

On Tesco's tiramisu dessert (printed on bottom): Do not turn upside down.

On Marks & Spencer Bread Pudding: Product will be hot after heating.

On Salisbury's peanuts: Warning: Contains nuts.

On an American Airlines packet of nuts: Instructions: Open packet. Eat nuts.

Caviar has long been the badge of upmarket dining, and still divides gourmets the world over. Given that caviar is merely fish eggs it is often denounced as being over-rated. Caviar has been revered for centuries, in places such as ancient Egypt, Greece, Persia and Rome. The huge price is the result of the difficulty of obtaining the right kind of sturgeon, which should be beluga, ossetra or sevruga. For years the majority of caviar has come from the Black Sea and the Caspian Sea, but Iranian caviar is exceptionally good and is gaining ground fast. Good caviar should be not too salty, and should smell like fresh salt water. It should have an unbroken glistening, thin outer membrane with distinct individual roe or eggs, and should be eaten from a horn spoon, so it is not tainted with the taste of metal.

Truffles are edible subterranean mushrooms that are hard to find, and therefore a much sought-after delicacy. Pungent tasting and rich-smelling, these fungi are roundish and semi-hard, and look like a brown, wrinkled root vegetable. Trained truffling pigs or dogs are used to find them, as only they can smell the pungent scent above ground

Saffron strands are the stamens of the saffron crocus, which are harvested, dried and then used in cooking. It is mainly grown in Spain and India, though was grown in the UK from the 15th to 18th century. Its considerable cost is because it is hard to obtain; to produce saffron, the stamens must be individually extracted, not an easy job considering the tiny size of the plant. To produce a pound of saffron you would need to individually hand-treat 25,000 stamens and each crocus provides only three stamens.

COOKING CONUNDRUMS

What does an anthropophagist eat?
Answer on page 144

FIRST PAST THE POST

Tasty-sounding winners of some of Britain's
key horse races:

1777	Bourbon	St Leger
1778	Hollandaise	St Leger
1785	Trifle	Oaks
1796	Ambrosio	St Leger
1808	Morel	Oaks
1837	Mango	St Leger
1855	Saucebox	St Leger
1822	Pastille	Oaks
1843	Poison	Oaks
1854	Mincemeat	Oaks
1856	Mince Pie	Oaks
1868	The Lamb	Grand National
1871	The Lamb	Grand National
1882	Dutch Oven	St Leger
1893	Mrs Butterwick	Oaks
1896	Persimmon	St Leger and Derby
1905	Cherry Lass	Oaks
1906	Spearmint	Derby
1916	Vermouth	Grand National
1924	Salmon-Trout	St Leger
1931	Sandwich	St Leger
1959	Oxo	Grand National
1966	Sodium	St Leger
1973	Red Rum	Grand National
1974	Red Rum	Grand National
1975	L'Escargot	Grand National
1977	Red Rum	Grand National

SONGS WITH A LITTLE FLAVOUR

American Pie – Don MacLean
Big Apple – Kajagoogoo
Black Coffee – All Saints
Breakfast in America – Supertramp
Breakfast in Bed – UB40 with Chrissie Hynde
Brown Sugar – Rolling Stones
Candy Man – Brian Poole and the Tremeloes
Cornflake Girl – Tori Amos
I Heard It Through the Grapevine – Marvin Gaye
Judge Fudge – Happy Mondays
Life is a Minestrone – 10cc

CULINARY LEGENDS

Alexis Soyer (1810–1858) was a French cook who fed some of the most important people of his time, but also used his talents to feed the poor. While working in Paris, he rose to become the deputy chef at the Ministry of Foreign Affairs, but after the July revolution of 1830, he moved to England, where he married an English actress. He was appointed head chef at the Reform Club from 1837 to 1850, where he installed the kitchens. These included a gas cooking range, which was unusual for the time, even for a large cooking establishment. In 1847, he was commissioned by the government to open kitchens in Dublin to help feed victims of the Irish famine, and he later served during the Crimean war as a dietary advisor to the British army, improving the rations and inventing more efficient ways to cook in the field. He wrote several books for both wealthy and impoverished gourmets – *The Gastronomic Regenerator* (1846), *The Poor Man's Regenerator* (1848) and *A Shilling Cookery for the People* (1854), the last of which sold a quarter of a million copies.

ESSENTIAL INVENTIONS

Ideas that changed the way we eat

Canned food: 1795
In the late 18th century, Napoleon promised 12,000 French francs to anyone who could come up with a method of preserving food that could be used by his armies while on campaign. French cook and inventor Nicolas Appert won the prize, though it took him 14 years to perfect his method. Using glass jars sealed with wax and wire, he found that if food is heated and sealed in an airtight container, it will not spoil.

The refrigerator: 1805
Artificial refrigeration was first demonstrated by William Cullen in Glasgow in 1748. But it took until 1805 for American inventor, Oliver Evans, to design the first refrigeration machine. The first actual refrigerator was built by Jacob Perkins in 1834.

The egg beater: 1884
African American, Willis Johnson of Cincinnati, Ohio, patented an improved mechanical egg beater on 5 February 1884. His device was more of an early mixing machine than just an egg beater, as it could mix eggs, batter, and other baker's ingredients.

The electric toaster: 1893
The first electric toaster was invented in 1893 in the UK by Crompton and Co and re-invented in 1909 in the US. In July, 1909, Frank Shailor of General Electric submitted his patent application for the D-12, considered the first commercially successful electric toaster. Charles Strite invented the modern, pop-up toaster in 1919.

Aluminium foil: 1910
Dr Lauber, Neher & Cie, Emmishofen was opened in Kreuzlingen, Switzerland. The plant was owned by JG Neher & Sons (aluminium manufacturers) and it was Neher's sons together with Dr Lauber who discovered

the endless rolling process and the use of aluminium foil as a protective barrier.

The kitchen blender: 1922
Stephen Poplawski invented the blender in 1922, as he was the first person successfully to put a spinning blade at the bottom of a tall container, which proved the winning combination.

The electric kettle: 1922
Arthur Leslie Large invented the electric kettle in 1922.

The cheese-slicer: 1927
On a hot summer day in Norway in 1927, Thor Bjørklund had his lunch break. On discovering four melted slices of cheese, he tried to separate them; first with his knife, then his saw, and finally with his plane – which worked beautifully. And the rest is history.

The Aga: 1929
Swedish scientist Gustaf Dalén saved thousands of lives with his work on lighthouse technology. His work involved the safe use of acetylene gas, so it is ironic that he was blinded in an experiment involving acetylene cylinders. Recovering at home, Dalén realised how badly designed the kitchen range was. Dalén set about improving its details, and the Aga cooker was launched in 1929.

Tupperware: 1947
Tupperware was invented by Earl Silas Tupper, a New Hampshire tree surgeon and plastics innovator, who began experimenting with polyethylene, a new material used primarily for insulation, radar and radio equipment.

The microwave: 1945
US electronics expert Percy Spencer was touring one of his laboratories at the Raytheon Company when he experienced a strange sensation, and noticed that the chocolate in his pocket had softened. He realised he was standing in front of a magnetron and his curiosity was aroused. The first microwave oven was sold in 1947, though it was too large for domestic use. The first counter-top microwave went on sale in 1967.

I'D LIKE TO TEACH
THE WORLD TO DRINK

In 2002, the most valuable product in the world was Coca-Cola, outstripping even Microsoft by having a brand value of $69,637,000,000. (McDonald's trailed in at number eight with a value of $26,375,000,000.) Coca-Cola was also the most advertised food or drink in the UK, as the company spent £16,497,785 on promoting their product. The next three brands on this advertising spend list were Guinness, Budweiser and Carling. The first food on the list, at number four, was the KitKat bar.

FOOD FOR THOUGHT

•In 2000, the food industry spent around £10.9 billion on chemical food additives to improve the colour, flavour, texture and shelf life of its products.

•Consumers in the developed world ingest between six and seven kilogrammes of food additives a year.

•Some of these additives are designed to prevent food poisoning and prolong the life of the food. However, the additives that prevent food from deteriorating account for only 1% of all additives in food. Around 90% are used for cosmetic reasons, to change the colour, flavour or texture of the food.

•There are 540 food additive compounds that are deemed safe for human consumption by regulatory bodies.

•Of the 540, 320 are accepted as reasonably safe. Doubts have been raised about the safety of 150 others. Seventy may cause allergic reactions and intolerance in some people and 30 could cause significant long-term damage.

TASTY CHILDHOOD TALES

The Adventures of Huckleberry Finn, Mark Twain
The Battle of Bubble and Squeak, Philippa Pearce
Charlie and the Chocolate Factory, Roald Dahl
The Chocolate War, Robert Cormier
Each Peach Pear Plum, Janet and Allan Ahlberg
The Great Big Enormous Turnip, Helen Oxenbury
Green Eggs and Ham, Dr Seuss
Garth Pig and the Ice Cream Lady, Mary Rayner
I Am The Cheese, Robert Cormier
James and the Giant Peach, Roald Dahl
Orlando the Marmalade Cat, Kathleen Hale
Peacock Pie, Walter de la Mare
The Peppermint Pig, Nina Bawden
The Piemakers, Helen Cresswell
The Story of Chicken Licken, traditional fairy tale
The Tale of the Pie and the Patty-Pan, Beatrix Potter
The Tale of Ginger and Pickles, Beatrix Potter
Cecily Parsley's Nursery Rhymes, Beatrix Potter

EXPERT ADVICE

How to tell if an egg is fresh

Once an egg has been laid, it has a limited shelf life, as the egg white and yolk slowly break down inside the shell. As this happens, air accumulates within the shell, so the older the egg, the more air is inside it. To test if an egg is fresh, place it in a deep bowl of water. If it lies on the bottom, it is fresh. If it stands on one end and bobs on the bottom of the bowl, it is older but still ideal for scrambling or hard-boiling. If the egg floats to the surface, it is probably rotten.

THE WAY WE WERE

From the household accounts of Lord William Howard's
steward at Naworth Castle in Cumberland (c.1619):

Bought of Mr Hall at St Luke's fair by my wyfe:

A quarter of c of reysons solis [sun raisins] ....xvi s iii d
c of fine currants..lii s
140 li of powder suger, at 13d....................vii li xi s viii d
One pound of mace and cloves ....1/2 li xii s
ii li of licorace ....xii d
One l of anyseeds ....x d
ii li of large cynomom.......................................vii s iiii d
x li of jurden [Jordan] almonds, at 16d.............xiii s iiii d
12 li of case pepper at 2s 4d ....xxxviii s
One loafe of suger of xiii li, xi ounces ....xvii s ii d
viii li of large ginger ....viii s
One pound of a case of nutmegs ....iiii s
One gallon of olives ....viii s
6 li of cappers [capers] ....viii s
2 li d. of wett sucket [sweets] ....iii s ix d
One pound of candied ginger ....iiii s
2 barrells for olives and sucketts ....ix d
saffron...xii d
Nutmeggs ....xxii d
Sanders [Indian wood for dyeing jellies]......................vi d

c = hundredweight; l and li = pounds (*liber* and *libri*);
s = shillings; d = pence

GILDING THE SAUSAGE

If you see the additive E175 in a list of ingredients, treat
that food with respect – the number denotes gold leaf, an
authorized additive for charcuterie, confectionery and
cake decorations.

CRÈME DE LA CRÈME

The expression *cordon bleu*, the byword for high-class cooking, originated with L'Ordre des Chevaliers du Saint-Esprit, the highest order of knighthood in France, which was created in 1578 by Henri III. These exalted knights wore a medal attached to a blue ribbon and their spectacular feasts became legendary throughout the country. The term, therefore, came to be used to describe outstanding chefs capable of preparing the very best feasts. The cooking school was founded in 1895, 'to promote the worldwide appreciation of gastronomy and to encourage excellence in the culinary arts'. There are now 22 Cordon Bleu schools in 12 countries around the world.

COOKING CONUNDRUMS

A man was walking down a road carrying a basket of eggs. As he walked he met someone who buys one-half of his eggs plus one-half of an egg. A little further he meets another person who buys one-half of his eggs plus one-half of an egg. Later he meets another person who buys one-half of his eggs plus one half an egg. At this point he has sold all of his eggs, and he never broke an egg. How many eggs did the man have to start with?

Answer on page 144

TOP TEN PASTAS

The UK's favourite pasta shapes in order of market share:

Spaghetti – 26%	Tagliatelle – 8.0%
Twists – 18%	Noodles – 7.1%
Assorted shapes – 13.5%	Macaroni – 6.3%
Lasagne – 9.2%	Tortellini – 2.5%
Shells – 9.0%	Cannelloni – 0.4%

OLD PICTURE, NEW CAPTION

*Despite repeated attempts to be rid of them, the professor
realised he still had a mouse problem.*

VENICE TREACLE

Venice treacle was a remedy against poison, developed
in Italy, and used across Europe until the 19th century.
Also known as theriac, it was an ancient remedy consisting of up to 70 drugs, pounded and mixed with honey.
Treacle has been used as an antidote to poison since
ancient times; the word treacle is thought to mean 'antidote to the bite of a wild beast'. The recipe for Venice
treacle spread all over the world and can be found in the
historical medical records of most countries. It is even
mentioned in Daniel Defoe's *Journal of the Plague Year*:
'Others think that Venice treacle is sufficient of itself to
resist the contagion… I several times took Venice treacle,
and a sound sweat upon it, and I thought myself well fortified against the infection.'

BIG EATERS

The largest item to be found on any menu is probably a roasted camel, which occasionally graces a Bedouin wedding feast. The whole dish consists of cooked eggs stuffed into fish, stuffed into a cooked chicken, which is stuffed into a roasted sheep's carcass, which is, finally, stuffed into the camel. A modern equivalent might be the Turducken, invented by a Louisiana chef in the 1960s; a chicken, duck and turkey are boned and laid out flat, with the turkey on the outside, then the duck and the chicken on top. All three birds are rolled up and sewn in place, and the whole is roasted slowly for up to 13 hours.

WHAT'S IN A NAME?

The original meaning of a few place names:

Anguilla – eel
Annapurna – abundant food
Aran Islands – kidney islands
Bangkok – region of olive trees
Bethlehem – house of bread
Bethphage – house of figs
Chicago – garlic place
Clonmel – meadow of honey
Coney Island – rabbit island
Dalmatia – young animal
Danube – river of sheep
Fair Isle – islands of sheep
Galapagos – giant tortoise
Grasse – fat
Harbin – place where fish is dried
Killarney – church of the sloes
Saskatoon – fruit of tree of many branches
Shiraz – good grape
Topeka – a good place to dig potatoes

TOP 10 COFFEE FACTS

• The word coffee comes from the Arabic, *qahwah*, a poetic word for wine. Coffee was first made from boiling the leaves, rather than roasting and grinding the beans. The first person to make coffee from beans is believed to have been an Islamic hermit called ad-Shadhili, around 1200 AD, in north Africa.

• Islamic alchemists believed that mixing coffee with milk caused leprosy.

• The coffee we buy is mostly either robusta or arabica. Arabica is considered a better quality.

• Coffee beans were first brought to Europe in 1615, by the Italians.

• The first coffee house in Europe was opened by a Turkish Jew, in Oxford, in 1650.

• Hazrat Shah Jamer Allah Mazarabi smuggled seven green coffee beans out of Mecca and took them to India. Taking 'live' beans out of the country was punishable by death. He planted them in Mysore, and single-handedly began the entire Indian coffee-producing industry. A seedling was taken from this plantation to Indonesia in 1696 by a Dutchman, which in turn began the long history of Indonesian coffee plantations of the 18th century.

• In Italy, coffee is sometimes drunk with a curl of lemon peel, sprinkling of grated lemon or orange peel; in Russia with a squeeze of lemon; in Morocco with whole black peppercorns; and in Ethiopia and Morocco with a pinch of salt.

• The first International Coffee Agreement took place at the United Nations in 1962.

• The National Institute on Drug Abuse claimed that, in the last recorded year, 5,000 Americans were killed by caffeine in one year.

• Fairtrade coffee now accounts for 18% of UK roast and ground coffee.

ELEVEN REPETITIVE FOODS

agar-agar – a vegetarian alternative to gelatine,
made from seaweed
al pil-pil – in Spain, anything cooked in
an olive oil and garlic sauce
alfalfa – when sprouted from seed,
a delicate salad vegetable
baba – cake made from leavened dough that is
steeped in rum after baking
coco – plum-like fruit from West Indies
and Central America
couscous – small grain made of wheat or barley
fufu – also called foufou, a starchy African
savoury pudding or thick porridge
pawpaw – another name for papaya
pili-pili – a small, hot African pepper
quinquina – a bitter wine-based
aperitif containing quinine
tartar – crystalline deposit left inside wine casks, which
when purified is used in baking as cream of tartar

GOING UNDERCOVER

The word 'cover', which now refers to a place setting at
table, has a slightly murky origin. Until the 15th century,
food was served under the cover of a white napkin,
which indicated to the diner that all precautions had been
taken to avoid the food being maliciously poisoned. Even
after this danger subsided, the word stuck and is still
routinely used in restaurants. In France during the Ancien
Regime, 'cover' was also used to distinguish the king's
meals; *au grand couvert* was a large banquet or formal
meal, *le petit couvert* was a simple meal that the king ate
with intimate friends, although it still consisted of three
courses and required 15 attendants to serve it.

REASONS TO STAY HUNGRY

Nineteen phobias that might spoil your appetite:

Acerophobia – fear of sourness
Alektorophobia – fear of chickens
Alliumphobia – fear of garlic
Arachibutyrophobia – fear of peanut butter sticking
to the roofof your mouth
Carnophobia – fear of meat
Deipnophobia – fear of dining and dinner conversation
Dipsophobia – fear of drinking
Emetophobia – fear of vomiting
Geumatophobia – fear of taste
Hedonophobia – fear of pleasure
Icthyophobia – fear of fish
Lachanophobia – fear of vegetables
Mageirocophobia – fear of cooking
Olfactophobia – fear of smell
Ostraconophobia – fear of shellfish
Panophobia – fear of everything
Phagophobia – fear of swallowing
Pnigophobia – fear of choking
Sitophobia – fear of food

IN LOVING MEMORY

The Alferd Packer Memorial Grill in the University of
Colorado was named not after a generous benefactor, nor
after an accomplished chef, but after a local murderer
who ate his victims. Alferd Packer was a prospector who
lived in the Rocky Mountains who split open the skulls
of his companions while they slept and ate their remains.
Caught in 1874 he was convicted and jailed for 18 years.
However, his story made him notorious rather than
reviled, and he found himself almost a curiosity on his
release. Tourists still visit his grave.

OLD PICTURE, NEW CAPTION

*Pickwick was unable to hide his disappointment
on learning that the steamed treacle pudding was
finished for the day.*

COOKING CONUNDRUMS

In France, what does AAAAA stand for?
Answer on page 144

GUESS WHO'S COMING TO DINNER?

One of the largest banquets ever served took place in
Paris on 22 November 1900. Emile Loubet, then
President of the Republic, invited 22,295 mayors from
across France to a Mayors' Banquet, with the intention of
reviving their republican spirit. The visiting dignitaries
were served a feast of Rouen duck loaf, fillet of beef
Bellevue, chicken from Bresse and ballotine of pheasant.
The waiters covered the four miles of tables on bicycles.

AVOCADO AMMUNITION

In a letter to *The Times*, 11 May 1989...

Sir – In paying tribute to the versatility of the avocado pear, your recent correspondents appear to have overlooked its military applications.

When I was employed in the Colonial Secretariat in Entebbe 30 years ago, there was a fruitful avocado tree in our garden, windfalls from which provided an arsenal of ammunition for the rival gangs in which our own children and those of our colleagues used to play in their games. Indeed the gang based on the other side of our garden fence was fittingly known and respected as the Mighty Pear-Balls.

The over-ripe, rotten avocado pear is singularly well adapted for use as a projectile in juvenile gang warfare. It is not lethal; it is exactly the right size and weight for throwing; its large stone provides the requisite solidity and mass; and in the event of a direct hit its explosive potential is spectacularly satisfying.

Yours faithfully,
John Champion

NOW PLEASE WASH YOUR HANDS

US cook Mary Mallon (1870-1938) is better known as Typhoid Mary, the first typhoid carrier to be identified in the US. Though immune to the disease herself, she was believed to have caused 51 cases of typhoid and three deaths by passing the disease on. She was forcibly isolated in a New York hospital from 1907-1910, and released only on the condition that she did not work as a cook. However, when typhoid broke out at two hospitals, she was found to be working in the kitchens and was isolated in hospital for the rest of her life.

WORLD'S MOST EXPENSIVE COOKBOOK

Cuoco Secreto di Papa Pio Quinto
('The Private Cook of Pope Pius V') by Bartolomeo
Scappi was first published in 1570. A surviving 1596
edition was offered for sale by bookseller Martayan Lan
in New York, priced US$11,500.

THE ORIGINS OF BREAD AND BUTTER

Between 5,000 and 12,000 years ago, man stopped chasing his food and began to herd and farm instead. Climatic changes at the end of the Ice Age encouraged more edible plants such as wheat to grow. As man learned to harvest food, and replant the seeds, he was able to settle in one place, build a home and develop his cooking skills. As raw wheat is indigestible, historians conclude that it was roasted, ground, mixed with water and made into cakes on hot stones, somewhere around 9000 BC. These 'flatbreads' survive today as pitta, nan, tortilla, chapatti and so on. It was the perfect food, as it could be made and eaten without containers or cutlery.

In the Middle Ages, trencher bread was used to make a plate for meat dishes, then the soggy remains were given to the dogs, or to the poor.

But what to put on the bread? Between 9000 BC and 6000 BC, man began to domesticate animals. This gave him meat and milk. As with flatbreads, milk in its natural and fermented state is still a part of almost every traditional diet, from yogurt to Indian dahi and the 'discovery' of milk was closely followed by the invention of butter. Incidentally, it is thought that the use of animal stomachs as containers for milk probably created the first cheese, as the rennet in a calf's stomach helps to make milk into cheese.

A CAUTIONARY LIMERICK

There was a young gourmet of Crediton
Who took pâté de foie gras and spread it on
A chocolate biscuit
He murmured 'I'll risk it'
His tomb bears the date that he said it on.

Anon

COOKING CONUNDRUMS

There are 10 volumes of cookbooks on a kitchen shelf.
Each book is two inches thick. The books are lined up in
order. A bookworm starts to eat its way through the
books, starting with the front cover of Volume One, and
finishing with the back cover of Volume 10. He eats in a
straight line, so how far does he travel?

Answer on page 144

A MATTER OF TASTE

If you thought that all you could taste was sweet, sour,
salty and bitter, rejoice – there is another taste to savour,
known as *umami*. In 1908, Professor Ikeda from the
University of Tokyo set out to find what made *kombu*,
the traditional Japanese seaweed broth, taste so delicious.
He narrowed it down to glutamic acid, or glutamate,
which gives food a rich, savoury taste best described as
mouthfulness. Ikeda called it *umami*, which roughly translated means 'deliciousness'. Parmesan is very high in
glutamate, for example, as are sundried tomatoes and
tomato paste. As other scientists became interested, they
discovered more substances that gave foods a hint of
umami, and these were found in foods such as dried
bonito flakes, shiitake mushrooms, fish sauce, meat and
vegetable extracts such as Marmite, soy sauce and many
other fermented products.

WHAT DO WE EAT?

In a 2003 survey of eating habits in the UK, volunteers aged 19-64 recorded their regular food intake. The results are not entirely surprising, but dieticians of a sensitive nature may want to look away now.

Percentage who ate the foods below at least once a week:

	Men	Women
white bread	93	89
vegetables	81	80
bacon/ham	77	64
cheese	78	73
wholemeal bread	33	39
bananas	49	56
apples/pears	49	54
citrus fruits	25	30
table sugar	60	48
chocolate	54	57
other confectionery	20	25
soft drinks	52	48
beer	66	24
wine	36	45
tea	77	77
coffee	72	70

Portions of fruit and vegetables eaten per day: men 2.7, women 2.9

Number who eat five portions of fruit and vegetables per day: men 13% women 15%

Men aged 19-24 who eat three or more portions of fruit and veg per day: 0%

Overall, men and women aged 19-24 were more likely than those aged 50-64 to have eaten breaded chicken pieces, burgers, kebabs, savoury snacks, pizza, chips, fizzy drinks and alco-pops, and less likely to have eaten fresh vegetables and fruit, wholemeal bread and oily fish.

WORLD'S LARGEST FOOD FIGHT

The fruity festival of La Tomatina is a week-long celebration with bonfires, fireworks, drinking and entertainment to honour Saint Louis, the patron saint of the town of Bunol near Valencia. In 2001, 38,000 people spent an hour throwing 120 tonnes of tomatoes at each other. At the end, the town is awash with tomato juice and squashed tomatoes. It takes place on the last Wednesday of August – and as if that weren't enough food, the night before is usually marked by a giant paella cook-off.

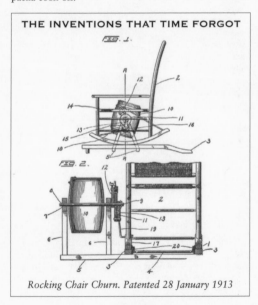

THE INVENTIONS THAT TIME FORGOT

Rocking Chair Churn. Patented 28 January 1913

FOOD FOR THOUGHT

Ten easy ways in which cooks can help to save the planet

1. Eat more organic foods To see how this could benefit you (and the farmers and the environment), see www.organicfoods.co.uk.

2. Be a responsible carnivore When you buy eggs, poultry, fish and meat that are certified organic, you can be sure that the animal has been protected by the highest standards of animal welfare.

3. Support local farmers Buy direct rather than via a middleman, so local farmers keep more of the profit. See www.farmers markets.net for your nearest market.

4. Buy seasonal Buy homegrown fruit and vegetables rather than imported produce.

5. Choose Fairtrade More of your money gets back to the supplier. See www.fair trade.org.uk to find out what's on offer.

6. Grow your own Growing your own fruit and vegetables is very satisfying (and if all you have is a windowbox, you can still grow herbs).

7. Conserve heat Keep oven doors closed and lids on pans to conserve heat when you're cooking.

8. Use the steam Cook vegetables in the steam from your rice or pasta pan – it saves energy, and conserves vitamins.

9. Make your garden happy Start a compost heap from kitchen waste, such as uncooked food, fruit, vegetables and coffee grounds. Add tissues, kitchen towel, egg cartons and cereal boxes. See www.compost.org.uk for more information.

10. Stay dust free Keep the condenser coils on your fridge free of dust (a dusty coil can increase energy consumption by 30%).

CAREFUL WITH THAT FISH BONE

During the most recent year for which figures
have been compiled:

- 3,946 people died from an accident in the home.
- 42,000 suffered an accident while eating or drinking.
- 14,000 suffered a non-fatal choking.
- Fish bones were the cause of 4,500 choking accidents.
- The next most common choking culprits were meat or poultry, followed by bones, sweets and coins.
- Under-fives were involved in more choking accidents than any other age group.
- The number of accidents due to choking fell sharply between 1992 and 1993, but is creeping back up.
- Around 41,000 people suffered a poisoning accident.
- Under-fives were involved in more poisoning accidents than any other age group.
- Around 102,000 people burned themselves at home.
- The key causes of household burns were kettles, steam, hot oil or fat and hot drinks.
- Under-fives were involved in more burn accidents than any other age group.

APRIL FOOD

The poisson d'Avril, the traditional French gift received on 1st April, derives from the 16th century, when Charles IX decreed that the New Year would begin on 1st January, instead of 1st April, as it had until then. His people were not amused, and took to sending each other worthless gifts on that day as mock New Year gifts. As the sun was in Pisces at the time, the fish shape seemed the obvious choice, and the French still give and eat chocolate, marzipan and sugar fish on April Fool's Day.

MORE SONGS WITH A LITTLE FLAVOUR

Marguerita Time – Status Quo
Milk and Alcohol – Dr Feelgood
Mistletoe and Wine – Cliff Richard
Money Honey – Bay City Rollers
Monster Mash – Bobby Pickett and the Crypt Kickers
Mouldy Old Dough – Lieutenant Pigeon
My Boy Lollipop – Millie
My Girl Lollipop – Bad Manners
No Milk Today – Herman's Hermits
Peaches – Stranglers
Red Red Wine – UB40
Strawberry Fields For Ever – The Beatles
Sugar and Spice – The Searchers
Sugar Baby Love – Rubettes
Sugar Town – Nancy Sinatra
Sweet Like Chocolate – Shanks and Bigfoot
Sweets for My Sweet – The Searchers
2 Pints of Lager and a Packet of Crisps Please –
Splodgenessabounds
Whiskey in the Jar – Thin Lizzy

LONDON ROADS OF FOOD

A tasty amble through the streets of London:

Artichoke Hill, SE5 • Bacon Grove, SE1 • Cheddar
Close, N11 • Duck Lane, W1 • Eatington Road, E10
Frying Pan Alley, E1• Grocer's Hall Court, EC2 • Ham
Yard, W1 • Ive Farm Lane, E10 • Juniper Lane, E6
Kitcat Terrace E3 • Lime Street, EC3 • Milk Street, EC2
Nutmeg Lane, E14 • Oat Lane, EC2 • Pudding Lane,
EC3 • Quorn Road, SE22 • Rye Lane, SE15 • Sugar
Bakers Court, EC3 • Tamarind Court, W8 • Vinegar
Street E1 • Walnut Gardens E15 • Yorkshire
[because you think of Pudding] Road, E14

CULINARY LEGENDS

Georges Auguste Escoffier (1846-1935), French chef *extraordinaire* was renowned for his superb cooking, the prestige of his patrons, his modernising influence on hotel cooking, in particular at the London Savoy, and the sheer length of his culinary career. Escoffier was chef at the Carlton Hotel in London, the Grande National Hotel in Lucerne, Switzerland, the Grand Hotel in Monte Carlo, the Savoy in London and the Ritz hotels in Paris and New York City. He wrote many authoritative books about cooking, and was made a Chevalier of the Legion of Honour in 1920. Emperor William II summed up Escoffier's career with the words: 'I am the Emperor of Germany, but you are the emperor of chefs.'

FIRST BEHEAD YOUR SHEEP

To help despairing housewives make palatable meals out of root vegetables, cheap cuts of meat and dried egg, Marguerite Patten published *The Victory Cookbook*, a triumph of optimism over resources. Alongside such recipes as Cabbage Casserole, Beetroot Fricassee and Mock Lemon Curd (cornflour, sugar, margarine and lemon squash) was Sheep's Head Roll. To summarise: blanch a sheep's head, tie it in a cloth (to keep the nourishing brains intact), place in pan with vegetables, spices, herbs and vinegar and simmer for one and a half hours. Remove the tongue and thinly slice. Remove the meat from the head, mince it and blend it with the 'softened' vegetables, and some breadcrumbs and flour. Form the meat into a long strip, place the tongue slices down the middle, roll it up and steam for one hour. Allow to cool, then serve cold. The recipe recommends that the cook 'add a little tomato ketchup or Worcestershire sauce to the meat mixture to give additional flavour'.

WHAT'S IN A NAME?

One way to become immortal is to have a
recipe named after you:

Beef Wellington – fillet steak encased in puff pastry named after The Duke of Wellington, prime minister and defeater of Napoleon.

Frangipane – a sweet custard flavoured with almonds and spices, named after Muzio Frangipani. He was a 16th century Italian marquis who created a perfume based on bitter almonds, which Parisian pastry cooks then tried to capture by adding almonds to the custard used for filling tartlets.

Garibaldi biscuit – a flat, chewy biscuit filled with currants, named after 19th century Italian commander Giuseppe Garibaldi.

Peach Melba – peaches, ice cream and raspberry sauce named after Dame Nellie Melba, and created for her by master chef Escoffier.

Sally Lunn – a large teacake made with a rich yeast mixture. Tradition has it that Sally was a pastry cook in 18th-century Bath, where she made and sold these buns in the streets.

Sauce Colbert – named after Jean-Baptiste Colbert, Louis XVI's treasurer, Sauce Colbert is a lemon sauce flavoured with parsley and Madeira.

Savarin – a large, ring-shaped, spongy cake made from a rich yeast mixture, soaked in a rum-flavoured syrup and filled with fruit and cream. Named after Jean-Anthelme Brillat-Savarin, historic French gourmet and writer on gastronomy.

Victoria Sandwich – a sponge cake sandwiched together with raspberry jam, named after Queen Victoria.

APPLES AND PEARS

Cockney rhyming slang on a food theme:

almond rocks – socks
apple fritter – bitter (beer)
apples and pears – stairs
bacon and eggs – legs
Bath bun – son
bees and honey – money
biscuits and cheese – knees
bladder of lard – card
bread and butter – gutter
bread and cheese – sneeze
Brussel sprouts – scouts
bubble and squeak – beak (magistrate)
butcher's [hook] – look
carving knife – wife
china plate – mate
chop sticks – six
cocoa – say so
crust of bread – head
currant bun – son
custard and jelly – telly
field of wheat – street
ginger beer – queer
greengages – wages
jam jar – car
kidney punch – lunch
loaf of bread – head
macaroni – pony
mince pies – eyes
old pot and pan – old man
peas in the pot – hot
plates of meat – feet
potatoes in the mould – cold
salmon and trout – stout

FOOD IN THE FIFTIES

The 1950s could be thought of as the culinary era of innocence – the calm before the storm of BSE, GM foods, microwave dinners and Chilean strawberries in January. The men who survived the war had reclaimed their jobs, women went back to the kitchen, and the birth rate soared. When rationing ended in 1954, life began to seem rosy once more. Fresh fruit and vegetables were almost entirely home-grown, so the nation ate seasonally, with the occasional imported exotic fruit such as bananas and pineapples. Housewives shopped at small specialist shops, buying meat from the butcher, cheese from the grocer and so on. They often shopped daily, as few homes had fridges at the beginning of the decade, and there were more local village shops. Most food was sold loose and was weighed out to order. Bread, milk, vegetables and other groceries were delivered to the door. Families spent around one-third of their income on food and drink (by 2001, it was only 16%). However, things were changing. As well as an end to rationing, the 1950s brought commercial television; TV's first celebrity chef, Fanny Cradock; Elizabeth David's *Mediterranean Food*; and the first self-service convenience store, opened by J Sainsbury in Croydon.

LUCKY FOOD

A few Japanese superstitions

Do not pass food from chopstick to chopstick; this is only done with the bones of the cremated body at funerals.

Do not stick your chopsticks into your food, especially not into rice, because at funerals chopsticks are stuck into the rice that is put onto the altar.

Do not lie down after eating: if you lie down immediately after eating, you will become a cow.

THE TASTE OF GUILT

On 31 December 1995, former French president François Mitterand invited his friends to what he knew would be his last feast, as he was dying from cancer. What surprised his friends was the nature of the meal. Mitterand had decided to go out in style, and despite being extremely ill, ordered a menu of oysters, foie gras, roast capon and, to finish, ortolan. Ornithologists will wince; the ortolan is a very tiny, endangered songbird, barely the size of a big toe, which is illegal to catch and certainly illegal to eat for dinner. Predictably this makes it a much-desired delicacy, and Mitterand decided that he had little to lose by breaking the rules.

The ritual of ortolan-eating dates back to Roman times; the birds are caught, kept in darkness and overfed to increase their size, then drowned in a quantity of Armagnac and roasted for a few minutes. The diner covers his head with an embroidered cloth and puts the bird whole into his mouth, leaving only the head, which he bites off. The bird is then chewed, whole, bones and all, for up to 15 minutes, as the diner savours every last morsel of its newly acquired fat. In a last act of gastronomic defiance, Mitterand ate two. He died a few days later.

EXTREME EATING

David Hirschkop may have developed the world's most dangerous food – Dave's Insanity Sauce. His homemade chilli sauce is so explosively potent that he uses only one drop in any recipe, and even at that concentration it got him banned from the annual National Fiery Food Show in Albuquerque after one taster suffered a mild heart attack. For fans of *The Simpsons*, it was the inspiration for the Guatemalan Insanity Sauce that gave Homer Simpson a funny turn in one memorable episode in 1997.

COOKING CONUNDRUMS

You throw away the outside and cook the inside.
Then you eat the outside and throw away the inside.
What did you eat?
Answer on page 144

SAY IT WITH FOOD

Twelve ways to say that it's all gone horribly wrong

**He's buttered his bread
on both sides**
He's been extravagant

**He has need now
of nothing but a
little parsley**
He's dead

**It's neither fish, flesh
nor good red herring**
Not one thing or
another, or not suitable
for anything. These
three foods were
considered food for
monks, food for
everyone, and food for
poor people respectively

It's not the cheese
It's not right; it doesn't
cut the mustard

My cake is dough
My projects have failed

To be done brown
To be deceived

**To eat the calf in the
cow's belly**
To count your chickens
before they're hatched

To pluck a pigeon
To take money off a
gullible person

To shoe the goose
To waste time on
pointless activities

The fat is in the fire
The cat's out of the bag

To take one's gruel
To accept one's
punishment

**Where the chicken got
the axe**
To get it in the neck

THE FOOD OF LOVE

The word 'aphrodisiac' comes from the name of the goddess of love, Aphrodite, although it is more commonly thought of as something that provokes lust rather than love. Whatever effect you're looking for, here are a few traditional favourites:

Asparagus has that all-important phallic shape, but is also rich in vitamin E, believed by some to stimulate production of our sex hormones and to be essential for a healthy sex life.

The heat in **chilli peppers** comes from capsaicin, a chemical that stimulates our nerve endings, raising our pulse, making us sweat and simulating a state of sexual arousal. Some believe that hot food also triggers the release of endorphins, chemicals that give us a natural high that is conducive to love-making.

Chocolate contains phenylethylamine, which creates a feeling of well-being and excitement similar to that experienced when making love. It also contains two stimulants, theobromine and caffeine. Research suggests that the amounts in chocolate are too low to make a difference. We say that Belgian truffles can provoke all kinds of interesting emotions.

Coffee contains caffeine, a stimulant. Also, sperm exposed to caffeine swim faster. However, in past eras, caffeine was thought to deprive the body of semen and render a man impotent.

Damiana, or wild yam, has traditionally been used as an aphrodisiac, and analysis shows that it contains chemicals that can increase sensitivity in the genitals. It is also used as an alternative remedy for hormone replacement, as it is believed to affect hormone levels in the body.

Some experimenters have used **gingko** to treat sexual dysfunction, possibly because it stimulates the release of nitric oxide. This widens the blood vessels of the genitals and erectile tissue.

Research shows that **oysters** are rich in zinc, a mineral required for the production of testosterone. Testosterone is believed to stimulate the female libido as well as the male. The texture and taste are also sup-

posed to have something to do with the oyster's aphrodisiac effect, via the imagination.

Although there is no scientific background, it is thought that the aroma and rarity of a **truffle** help to create a degree of stimulation. As Brillat-Savarin wrote: 'The truffle is not a true aphrodisiac, but in certain circumstances it can make women more affectionate and men more attentive.'

THE INVENTIONS THAT TIME FORGOT

Machine for the electric extraction of poisons.
Patented 5 July 1898

FULL OF BEANS

Beans are one of the world's oldest foods. They're full of protein, vitamins, minerals, carbohydrates and fibre, they're low in fat and salt, contain no cholesterol, can be stored for a long time and they're cheap. Try a new flavour today:

black beans: black-skinned kidney beans with white flesh, common in Latin America

black-eyed peas: small and creamy white with a black spot, easily digestible

borlotti beans: long pale pink or beige Italian beans, creamy and slightly sweet

butter beans: flat, white beans, soft floury texture

flageolet beans: delicate pale green or white, gourmet kidney beans

Greek beans: large flat beans with no skin, good for puréeing

large white kidney beans: one of the largest beans, flat, white and buttery, much used in Spain and France

pinto beans: small kidney bean with pink, speckled skin, used in south-west USA and Latin America

red kidney beans: one of the most familiar beans, used in chilli con carne

small white haricot (navy) beans: typically used in French cassoulet and by Mr Heinz for his baked beans in tomato sauce

FIRST 10 THINGS YOU LEARN AT LEITH'S

The Leith School of Cookery in London is one of the UK's top culinary training schools. Here are the first 10 things they teach their aspiring cooks:

1. Knife skills – how to finely dice an onion and reduce a carrot to batons
2. How to write a cook's timeplan (what to do in what order and how long it takes)
3. Emulsions – eg how to make mayonnaise
4. Seasoning – how to season correctly, starting with vegetable soup
5. Eggs – the perfect omelette
6. Pastry – the secrets of shortcrust
7. Custard – how to make crème anglaise
8. The importance of presentation (demonstrated by making a fruit salad)
9. Stock – making clear chicken stock
10. How and why to brown meat

TABLE MANNERS

In medieval times, dagger-shaped knifes and spoons were being used as cutlery in Europe. But forks had not yet caught on, and food was for the most part eaten with the fingers. This made hygiene somewhat important, especially as dishes were set in the middle of the table for everyone to dip into. A number of etiquette books at the time felt it necessary to recommend that diners avoid putting their fingers into their ears or noses, or scratching their heads or private parts in between forays into the stew. The same writers also felt moved to warn people not to poke around on the central platter looking for the nicest bit of meat, nor to put gnawed bones back in the dish. Instead, they should throw them on the floor, like everyone else.

GIVE US OUR DAILY... MILK

Average weekly consumption of food per person
in the UK in 2002:

Milk and cream 2,140g
Meat/meat products 966g
Flour and other cereals (excl bread) 788g
Fresh fruit..745g
Fresh veg (excl potatoes) 732g
Bread 720g
Fresh potatoes 707g
Processed vegetables (inc potatoes)...........................546g
Processed fruit and nuts 375g
Fats..86g

STORM IN A TEACUP

The Boston Tea Party is history's great misnomer; it was
fuelled by anger, started a war and there were no fairy
cakes involved. By 1773 Britain repealed all 'unfair' taxes
on goods imported by America apart from the one on
tea, which they kept, largely to make the point that they
had the right to impose such taxes on their colonies. In
protest, some American ports began to turn away tea
deliveries from Britain. In retaliation, the British began to
export tea to the US at so low a price they thought it
would be bound to sell. Instead, the Americans rebelled.
In December 1773, a group of American radicals dressed
as Mohawk Indians boarded a vessel in Boston Harbour
and threw its cargo of tea overboard. Britain ordered the
port closed until the cost was repaid. Their intransigence
led to the meeting of the First Continental Congress (all
of the American colonies bar Georgia) in 1774, which
banned all imports from and exports to Britain. Then in
1776, America declared its independence from Britain,
and the American War of Independence began.

COOKING CONUNDRUMS

You use a knife to slice my head.
You weep beside me when I am dead.
What am I?
Answer on page 144

FAMOUS GLUTTONS

Maximinus the Thracian was said to be able to drink
an amphora of wine and consume 40 to 60lbs of meat
at a single sitting.

Clodius Albinus, an esteemed Roman Emperor, could
eat 500 figs, a basket of peaches, 10 melons, 20lbs of
grapes, 100 warblers and 400 oysters in one meal.

Vitellius, another Roman Emperor, had a favourite
dish that consisted of pike liver, pheasant brains,
peacock brains, flamingo tongues and lamprey roe,
scarce ingredients that had to be gathered from all
corners of his Empire. He 'thought nothing of snatching
lumps of meat or cake off the altar, almost out of the
sacred fire, and bolting them down.'

Philoxenos, a great epicure, was said by Aristotle to wish
he had a longer neck, to enjoy the food for longer.

Louis XIV ate so much at his wedding feast that he
was incapacitated.

Duke Ellington, jazz musician, claimed to enjoy
eating until it hurt.

Monsieur Creosote exploded at the end of the
restaurant scene in Monty Python's *The Meaning of Life.*
The wafer-thin mint that proved fatal has since become
a British catchphrase.

Elvis Presley in his later years consumed too much of
everything, and died of heart failure aged 42. One of his
favourite meals consisted of a whole loaf of bread filled
with peanut butter, jam and bacon.

I'LL EAT MY HATTE

The origin of this phrase has nothing, in fact, to do with headgear. Hattes have been found in early European cookbooks, although their ingredients and preparation are disputed. The acknowledged recipe included eggs, veal, dates, saffron and salt but could also include tongue, kidney, fat, honey, rosemary and cinnamon. It was generally thought to be an unappetising dish, and so the promise by someone that they would eat a hatte if they were wrong showed how sure they were that they would be proven right.

SPOILT FOR CHOICE

A few things you may find in store-bought food...

Colourings – used to modify the colour of a product

Preservatives – added to food to prevent the growth of harmful micro-organisms, and so allow food to last longer while being transported. Include sulphur dioxide, sulphites, sodium nitrate, sodium nitrite, potassium nitrate, potassium nitrite

Antioxidants – added to food to stop oils and fats from going rancid

Anti-caking agents – used to stop the absorption of water and to prevent powdered mixtures sticking together

Emulsifiers and stabilisers – used to make sure that water and oil stay mixed together

Thickeners – used to thicken a product

Flavour enhancers – chemicals to improve the flavour of the food. There are 36 compounds of flavour enhancer with the most commonly known one being monosodium glutamate (MSG)

THE REAL CAPTAIN BIRDSEYE

Clarence Birdseye (1886–1956) was the creator of the modern frozen food industry.

During World War I, Birdseye lived in Labrador with his wife, where he observed the people of the Arctic preserving fresh fish and meat in barrels of sea water; which were quickly frozen by the arctic temperatures, Clarence Birdseye concluded that it was the rapidity of the freezing that made food retain its freshness when thawed and cooked months later. In 1923, with an investment of $7 for an electric fan, buckets of brine and cakes of ice, Clarence Birdseye invented a system of packing fresh food into waxed cardboard boxes and flash-freezing it under high pressure.

The Goldman-Sachs Trading Corporation and the Postum Company (later the General Foods Corporation) bought Clarence Birdseye's patents and trade marks in 1929 for $22 million. The first quick-frozen vegetables, fruits, seafoods, and meat were sold to the public for the first time in 1930 in Springfield, Massachusetts, under the tradename Birds Eye Frosted Foods. The first individual frozen meal – chicken fricassee and steak – was sold in 1939.

I WOULDN'T EAT THAT IF I WERE YOU

The viscera of Japanese *abalone* (sea snails) can harbour a poisonous substance, which causes a burning, stinging, prickling and itching over the entire body. The symptoms do not arise until the sufferer is exposed to sunlight, but if the sea snails are actually eaten outdoors in sunlight, the symptoms occur immediately and may even cause skin lesions. It is believed the toxin may come from seaweed ingested by the abalone. Nevertheless, sea snails are a delicacy in Japan and China.

TIS AN ILL WIND

According to Reay Tannahill's *Food in History*, the aspect of dining etiquette that has attracted the most comment throughout history is that of breaking wind. In China, farting in public was specifically banned as long ago as the 6th century BC. In India 400 years later, etiquette regarding meeting the king forbade anyone to 'indulge in loud laughter where there is no joke, nor break wind'. Emperor Claudius took a different line, allowing his fellow diners to release their intestinal gases, as he feared that restraining the impulse might do some damage – which suggests that until then it had indeed been banned.

A BRIEF HISTORY OF CHOCOLATE

• Chocolate was first consumed by the Aztecs and their predecessors in the south Americas as a bitter, savoury drink made by roasting and pounding the cocoa beans, and adding flavourings such as chilli and pepper. The Aztec word for chocolate was *xocolatl*, meaning 'bitter water'.

• The cocoa tree was so valuable that the seeds were used as currency. A slave cost around 100 cocoa beans, and the services of a 'public woman' cost 10 cocoa beans – the same price as a rabbit.

• Columbus 'discovered' the cocoa bean in 1502, but when he took it home to King Ferdinand, the King showed no interest. The discovery is credited instead to the Spanish conquistador Hérnando Cortés. After landing in Mexico in 1519, he took the cocoa bean back to Spain, where vanilla and sugar (also new to Spain) were added to the bitter drink.

• The botanist Linnaeus named the cocoa tree *Theobroma cacao*, meaning 'food of the gods'. The cocoa bean includes theobromine, a very mild stimulant that triggers the release of endorphins in the brain, which in turn create feelings of euphoria, particularly of love and arousal. Casanova recommended a cup of hot chocolate as a 'restorative', and preferred it to champagne.

• When Anne of Spain married Louis XIII of France in 1651, she brought her own chocolate with her, and a maid, La Molina, whose sole task was to prepare it.

Pope Pius V thought hot chocolate so disgusting that there was no need to ban it during Lent.

• In mid-17th century Spain, the Bishop of Chiapa was allegedly poisoned by a cup of hot cocoa after he tried to ban women from drinking hot chocolate in church.

• Chocolate arrived in England in the 1650s and was served in coffee-houses as well as in chocolate houses such as Whites. In an effort to prevent the rowdy behaviour and gambling that these places encouraged, Charles II tried to suppress the coffee-houses in a proclamation in 1675, but it was largely ignored.

• Sir Hans Sloane, physician to Queen Anne and Samuel Pepys, is credited with first adding milk rather than water to hot chocolate. He sold his recipe to an apothecary, and it later passed into the hands of the Cadbury brothers.

• Solid chocolate was first created in 1819 by Francois-Louis Cailler.

• In 1847, Fry's became the first British company to make solid chocolate bars for eating, having discovered independently of Cailler how to solidify the mixture.

• Cadbury's supplied 1,500lbs chocolate to Scott's expedition to the Antarctic on his discovery tour in 1901-1904.

• Quality Street chocolates, launched in 1936, were named after a play by JM Barrie.

• Milton Snavely Hershey, the American confectionery millionaire, inspired Roald Dahl's *Willy Wonka*.

COOKING SAINT

Macarius the Younger, also known sometimes as
Macarius of Alexandria, is the patron saint of
confectioners, cooks and pastry chefs. He was born
in the early 4th century in Alexandria, Egypt and was
a successful merchant in fruits, sweets and pastries.
However, when he converted to Christianity, he gave
up his business in 335 AD to be a monk in the Thebaid,
Upper Egypt. After several years, he travelled to Lower
Egypt, was ordained, and lived in a desert cell with other
monks, practising severe austerities. For seven years –
perhaps to erase the indulgences of his original profession
– he lived on raw vegetables dipped in water with a few
crumbs of bread, moistened with drops of oil on feast
days. He submitted himself to a number of deprivations
and trials, including 20 days and 20 nights in the desert
without sleep, burnt by the sun in the day and frozen
by bitter cold at night; and six months living naked in
the marshes, beset by vicious blood-sucking flies and
mosquitoes. The experience left him so deformed that
when he returned to the monks, they could recognise
him only by his voice. He died around 401 AD.

YOU NEVER CAN TELL

Jerome Irving Rodale, the founding father of the
organic food movement, creator of *Organic Farming
and Gardening* magazine, and founder of Rodale Press,
a major publishing corporation, died while discussing
the benefits of organic foods on a TV chat show. Rodale
was 72 when he appeared on the *Dick Cavett Show* in
January 1971. Part way through the interview, he
dropped dead in his chair from a heart attack. He had
claimed 'I'm going to live to be 100 unless I'm run down
by a sugar-crazed taxi driver.' The show was never aired.

GREATER GRAINS

Grains have been the staple diet of human beings for over 10,000 years, yet we are surprisingly conservative about trying new varieties. So if you're bored with pasta and rice, try a few of these:

Buckwheat – this tiny triangular seed is rich in rutin, which strengthens blood vessels, and is a good source of protein

Farro – an ancient grain used by the Greeks, not unlike brown rice but with larger, firmer grains

Freekeh – a traditional middle Eastern grain made from roasted green wheat, with a smokey, nutty taste; high in protein and fibre

Kamut – an ancient Egyptian grain that is high in protein, vitamins and minerals, and a rich, buttery flavour

Maize – gluten-free, so ideal for coeliacs; the grain with which polenta is made

Millet – regarded by many as the most nutritious food in the world; high in protein, low in starch, easily digested, rich in silicon which is good for hair, skin, teeth and nails; and gluten-free

Pearl barley – a small rounded grain like wheat or pudding rice, this ancient Roman grain was the food of gladiators. Contains calcium and potassium and can help to lower cholesterol levels

Quinoa – a tiny, bead-shaped grain, pale gold, easy and quick to cook, with a firm, crunchy texture; rich in protein, amino acids, B vitamins and fibre

Spelt – an ancient grain that is mentioned in the Bible; high in protein with a light and nutty flavour

Although Amelia was known for her impeccable manners, she was not to be trusted with a bowl of sticky toffee pudding.

STRANGE DIETS

Some people like to eat dirt. White kaolin clay has been a foodstuff for certain people for centuries, and is treasured for its flavour with the same enthusiasm that is reserved for truffles. In Mexico, clay tablets replace wafers in an annual religious celebration and some African Americans send packets of clay to expectant mothers. Australian aborigines make a white clay loaf wrapped in leaves and baked; and the Kai people in Papua New Guinea string small balls of clay on a skewer like a kebab and cook them over an open fire. Cheap, delicious and filled with minerals, kaolin clay comes in four varieties: red, white, black and the rarest blue, which contains tiny air bubbles that massage the palate like champagne when eaten.

MORE FILMS FOR FOODIES

The Atomic Café
Attack on a Bakery
The Breakfast Club
Breakfast in Bed
The Butcher's Wife
The Cook, The Thief, His Wife and Her Lover
Diner
Eat Drink Man Woman
Gas, Food, Lodging
The Man Who Came to Dinner
Naked Lunch
The Ploughman's Lunch
Steaming

READ, LEARN AND INWARDLY DIGEST

The human digestive system is around 26–33ft long.

The digestive system consists of five parts: mouth, oesophagus, stomach, small intestine and large intestine.

It takes six seconds for liquid and 15 seconds for food to reach the stomach from the mouth.

The epiglottis prevents food from going into your lungs when you eat.

Food is digested in the mouth, stomach and small intestine; the large intestine deals with waste.

The acid in your stomach is hydrochloric.

The human stomach must produce a new layer of mucus every two weeks or it will digest itself.

The stomach capacity is about 2–2.5 pints

It takes from one to five hours to digest a meal.

FIT THAT IN YOUR SHOPPING TROLLEY

The grocery list for the coronation feast of Pope Clement
VI in May 1344 read as follows:

15 sturgeon
60 pigs
68 barrels of lard and salted meat
80 saumées (each consisting of 500 loaves of bread)
101 calves
118 cows
300 pike
914 kids
1,023 sheep
1,446 geese
1,500 capons
3,043 fowls
7,428 chickens
50,000 tarts (requiring 3,250 eggs)

Also required were 300 jugs, 5,500 pitchers, 2,500 glass
flagons, 5,000 glasses and 2,600 drinking bowls. These
last items were hired rather than bought.

A STRANGE LOVE OF CUSTARD

Director Stanley Kubrick always intended his film *Dr
Strangelove*, released in 1964, to end in a huge custard
pie fight between the Russians and the Americans in
the War Room (which is why you can see a huge table
of food in the final version). The footage was shot, but
Kubrick decided that it was too farcical to fit in with the
rest of the film. Another reason was that, as President
Muffley took a pie in the face, he fell down, and General
Turgidson cried 'Gentlemen! Our gallant young president
has just been struck down in his prime!' The scene was
cut, because of sensitivity over the assassination of JFK.

MEAT THE NEIGHBOURS

Sawney Bean (c. 1400) plumbed the depths of human depravity to an extent not seen before or since. With a female partner, he took up residence in a seaside cave in Scotland and lived by robbing, murdering and then eating his victims. His family – which grew to include 14 children and 34 grandchildren, all the result of incest – joined in, helping with the murder, dismemberment, pickling and salting of human flesh. If, as often happened, they built up a surplus, they would simply throw any spare limbs into the sea. It was assumed that the Beans had consumed around 1,000 victims before the king himself led a search to hunt down the culprits. The entire family was seized and executed without trial.

SUFFER THE LITTLE CHILDREN

Pity the Victorian child if its mother believed the dietary advice given in Pye Henry Chavasse's *Advice to Mothers on the Management of their Offspring* (1844).

'New potatoes are acceptable, but old potatoes, well-cooked and mealy, are the best a child can have,' he claimed. Chevasse recommended that the under-10s break their fast with warm milk poured over stale bread (at least seven days old), and that they should not be given sweets or green vegetables, as both were little better than poison. The over-10s could drink weak beer and eat a little mutton, but not pork or beef. Conscientious parents took his advice to heart and fed their offspring a grim diet, including gruel made from ground-up biscuits, flour and milk. Chevasse maintained that 'meat, potatoes and bread, with hunger for their sauce, is the best and indeed should be the only dinner they should have'. Modern parents can only conclude that he didn't like children and wanted all the biscuits for himself.

WORTH HIS SALT

You might think that salt would be the cheapest
and simplest thing on the table, but not so. The
varying taste and texture of different salts is a hotly
debated topic among gastronomes, and the world's
finest salt is currently deemed to be Oshima Island
Blue Label Salt. It comes from the highly salted waters
around this remote Japanese island and can be bought
only by members of the very exclusive Blue Salt Club,
of which US food critic and culinary detective Jeffrey
Steingarten claims to be the only American member.
The salt, not surprisingly, is very expensive. Steingarten
admits in his book *It Must've Been Something I Ate*:
'I use it infrequently, so as not to squander it all before
next year's harvest. In fact, I don't use it at all.
How chic is that?'

A GOOD GRILLING

The word barbecue probably comes from *barbacoa*,
a Haitian word meaning grill, although another theory
suggests that it arose from the French phrase *de la barbe
à la queue* (from beard to tail), referring to a whole
animal being roasted. The barbecue and its many outdoor
derivatives, from the Hawaiian luau to the Japanese
hibachi grill, are popular the world over, possibly because
we love its simple, barbarian nature, and because a whole
roasted animal was for so long a central part of any
celebratory feast. Indeed, most people in the UK (84%)
choose to use charcoal on their barbecue rather than gas,
which is much simpler and more reliable, but takes away
all the fun of building a fire. In the UK, barbecuing is a
major leisure activity: nearly 50% of households own a
barbecue grill of some kind, and it was estimated that in
2003, we held a total of around 54 million barbecues.

COOKING CONUNDRUMS

Who is the larger: Methuselah, Salmanazar or Balthazar?
Answer on page 144

THE SECRET TO PERFECT TURKEY

If you are stumped by the annual task of roasting a turkey, Peter Barham, a physicist from Bristol University, claims to have come up with the perfect formula for cooking turkey. He believes that his heat-transfer equation accounts for every relevant variable, including the difference in temperature between fridge and oven.

It also accounts for the ratio of the specific heat of the turkey to the specific heat of the air, and the radius, girth and physical geometry of the turkey.

While breast meat benefits from cooking at a high temperature to bring out the flavour, legs and wings are better cooked for longer at lower temperatures. This means that if the cooking time is based on weight this is likely to result in part of the bird

being undercooked and part overcooked or burnt. 'The main problem is that different muscle groups on the breast, wings and legs benefit from different cooking times and temperatures,' said Dr Barham.

The scientist says his formula shows how to calculate the complete temperature profile of the turkey at all times, but as the formula is hard for a domestic cook to apply, it may be best simply to take note of his conclusion: 'The best method is to split the bird into separate pieces and cook the breast, legs and wings separately.'

However, if you must cook the bird whole, Dr Barham suggests that you cover the breast with aluminium foil to keep the legs and wings cooler than the rest of the bird, but still heated sufficiently.

WEBSITES FOR A BETTER DIET

www.bareingredients.com
A guide to what's in season in the northern and southern hemisphere, plus articles on healthy eating.

www.bigbarn.co.uk
Search for local producers and read about healthy eating, food campaigns and other food news, plus food facts about what's good for you.

www.fairtrade.org.uk
Remind yourself which coffee, chocolate, marmalade and other foods help to support farmers across the world.

www.finefoodworld.co.uk
Where to find fine food awards and fine food suppliers.

www.foodcomm.org.uk
The campaign for food safety in the UK.

www.foodlink.org.uk
Useful advice on food safety for conscientious cooks.

www.foodloversbritain.com
The website for fresh foodies, as it champions the UK farmer, the small producer and the buyer of good quality food. Seasonal foods are highlighted with recipes to match, and you can search for local producers.

www.foodstandards.gov.uk
Lots of facts and figures on nutrition, food safety, healthy eating and seasonal foods Less earnest than it sounds, this is packed with information and even a few jokes...

www.nutrition.org
Nutritional facts and figures

www.soilassociation.org
The website of the Soil Association, champion of organic foods.

www.slowfood.com
The website of an organisation devoted to the proper appreciation of good food in the face of an onslaught of its enemy: (boo, hiss) fast food.

www.thecarf.co.uk
The website for the Campaign for Real Food.

ORGANIC WORLD

Who buys the most organic food?

Country	GB£ per head in 2000
Denmark	61.34
Switzerland	51.46
Austria	26.41
Sweden	24.25
Netherlands	20.57
Germany	16.42
USA	14.09
France	11.45
Japan	10.64
New Zealand	8.32
UK	8.26
Australia	4.91

WORLD CLASS PORRIDGE

Every year in Carrbridge in Inverness-shire, the villagers uphold the standards of Scottish porridge by holding the Golden Spurtle World Porridge Championships. The prize is awarded to the entrant who makes the best traditional porridge using only water, oatmeal and salt – although they can choose from pinhead, coarse, medium or fine oatmeal. There is also a Speciality Porridge section for more creative recipes, which can use non-traditional ingredients such as fruit. Entrants must make a pint of porridge for the judges, who award marks for consistency, colour and taste. It is assumed that entrants will bring their own favourite porridge pan and spurtle (stirrer). Pre-soaking is allowed, but oat flakes are forbidden (the oatmeal must be untreated). As well as the Golden Spurtle Challenge Trophy and the coveted title of World Porridge Making Champion, the winner receives a weekend at a luxury hotel, which includes, presumably, a hearty breakfast.

WHO WAS JACK THE TREACLE EATER?

In rural Somerset stands a delightful folly on the edge of the Barwick Estate, marking one of the estate's boundaries. At the edge of a field is a roughly built archway, topped by a crenellated tower entered by an impossibly small door. Perched on the top of the tower is a carefree looking figure: Jack the Treacle Eater. There are two explanations for his name: first, that Jack was a murderer being sheltered by his wife, who – because she worked in Barwick House kitchens – could smuggle him food, which was mostly treacle. The second is that Jack was employed at Barwick House as a runner to carry messages to London, and was fed on a diet of treacle to give him energy for his task. As London is about 125 miles away, this seems unlikely, and certainly nutritionally unsound. The sugar crash would have kicked in before he got as far as Salisbury.

WHAT'S THE DIFFERENCE?

A conserve is much more than mere strawberry jam:

Conserves: Like jam, containing whole or pieces of fruit, but with a slightly softer set

Fruit butter: Thick preserve made from fruit purée and sugar, often with spices added

Fruit cheese: Made as fruit butter but cooked to a thick, firm consistency

Fruit curd: Fruit juice and zest mixed with sugar, butter and eggs

Jam: Made from fruit pulp or pieces, and a syrup made with the fruit juice and sugar

Jellies: Clear preserve made from the strained juice of cooked fruit, with sugar added

Marmalades: Jam made with citrus fruit and containing pieces of peel

STRANGE DIETS

A 78-year-old Chinese woman was reported in the *South China Morning Post* in 2003 to have eaten around 10 tonnes of soil over the past 70 years. Hao Fenglan from Zhangwu county in northern China began eating mud and dirt at the age of eight, and claimed to feel physical discomfort if she did not eat dirt at least once a day. The newspaper reported that the diet seemed to have done her little harm, as she appeared to be in good health.

FOOD FOR THOUGHT

• In the UK in 1980, 8% of men and 6% of women were obese. By 1995 this had risen to 16% of men and 18% of women. By 2001, the figures were 21% of men and 23% of women.

• In 1990, 5% of six to 15 year-olds were obese. In 2001, 16% of six to 15-year-olds were obese. In 1998, 9% of preschool children were obese.

• If obesity in the UK continues to increase at its current rate, by 2020 one-third of all adults, one-fifth of boys and one-third of girls will be obese.

• Obesity causes about 30,000 deaths in the UK, through conditions such as heart disease, stroke and diabetes. We spend £500 million a year treating obesity and related problems.

EXPERT ADVICE

To make perfect pastry, the secret is to keep everything very cold: and that means the ingredients, the utensils and your hands. Use ice water, cold butter and a very cold bowl (metal stays colder than ceramic). Wash your hands in cold water, and repeat if they warm up as you work. Handle the ingredients as little as possible, and leave the pastry to chill and rest in the fridge before you roll it out. It will be as light as a feather.

ART GOOD ENOUGH TO EAT

The Absinthe Drinker – Manet
Around the Fish – Klee
At the Bar – Toulouse-Lautrec
Belshazzar's Feast – Rembrandt
The Cornfield – Constable
Le Déjeuner sur l'Herbe – Manet
The Dinner Table – Matisse
Girl Drinking Wine with a Gentleman – Vermeer
The Last Supper – Dali, Holbein the Younger, Leonardo
da Vinci (among many others)
The Luncheon – Manet
The Luncheon of the Boating Party – Renoir
The Milkmaid – Millet
An Old Woman Cooking Eggs – Velázquez
The Pantry – Hooch
The Potato Eaters – Van Gogh
St Mawes at the Pilchard Season – Turner
The Soup – Picasso
Still Life with Gingerpot – Mondrian
Sunflowers and Pears – Gauguin
Tuna Fishing – Dali
Woman with Pears – Picasso
Women with Mangoes – Gauguin

COOKING CONUNDRUMS

In a marble hall white as milk
Lined with skin as soft as silk
Within a fountain crystal-clear
A golden apple doth appear.
No doors there are to this stronghold,
Yet thieves break in to steal its gold.
What is it?
Answer on page 144

It is to be noted that in some far-off countries, the natives are still unaware of the invention of cutlery.

WAS HE A GOOD EGG?

Humpty Dumpty was depicted as an egg in Lewis Carroll's Alice books, but the nursery rhyme does not actually say he's an egg, so it is unclear when and why it was first assumed. However, there are many theories about the origin of the nursery rhyme, the most popular of which has been that Humpty represented King Richard III, who fell from his horse in the Battle of Bosworth Field and was hacked to pieces. But the tourist board of East Anglia firmly maintains that Humpty was a powerful cannon used during the Civil War, which was mounted on top of the Wall Church in Colchester to defend the city in the summer of 1648.

CULINARY LEGENDS

Jean Anthelme Brillat-Savarin (1775-1826) is perhaps France's best-known gastronome. He gained a love of food from his mother, an accomplished *cordon bleu* cook, but chose law as his profession, although he also studied medicine and chemistry. His best-known work consists of eight volumes and its full title in English is *The Physiology of Taste, or Meditation on Transcendent Gastronomy, a Work Theoretical, Historical, and Programmed*. It combines science and history with gastronomic meditations. on such subjects as digestion, sleep, obesity and thinness, gourmands, appetite, fasting and the theory of frying.

FOUR AND TWENTY BLACKBIRDS
BAKED IN A PIE

Cooks in wealthy households in the late Middle Ages spent a lot of time on presentation,. Occasionally their dishes were designed to be more entertaining than edible. This recipe, roughly translated, is one example:

Make the coffin [piecrust] of a great pie. In the bottom make a hole as big as your fist, or bigger if you will. Let the sides of the coffin be somewhat higher than ordinary pies. Which done, put it full of flour and bake it, and being baked, open the hole in the bottom and take out the flour. Then [taking] a pie of the bigness of the hole in the bottom of the coffin, you shall put it into the coffin, and put into the coffin around the pie as many small live birds as the empty coffin will hold... And this is to be done at such time as you send the pie to the table, and set before the guests: where, uncovering or cutting up the great lid of the pie, all the birds will fly out, which is to delight and pleasure show to the company. And that they be not altogether mocked, you shall cut open the small pie.

A NICE JIM SKINNER

Should you find yourself in a Cockney caff, here's how to order your food...

bread – Uncle Fred
butter – stammer and stutter
cake – Sexton Blake
cheese – stand at ease
dinner – Jim Skinner
fish – Lilian Gish
fork – Duke of York
gravy – army and navy
kipper – Jack the Ripper
liver – cheerful giver
pickles – Harvey Nichols
soup – loop the loop
steak and kidney – Kate and Sydney
supper – Tommy Tucker
tea – you and me
water – fisherman's daughter

And finally...
bill – Jack and Jill (or Beecham's pill)

FOOD FOR THOUGHT

A 2003 study by mineralogist David Thomas concluded that nutrient levels in the UK's fruit and vegetables have fallen significantly in the last 50 years. In the same period, the sugar content of some fruits had almost doubled. The researcher connect the decline in nutrients to the modernising of farming techniques that occurred over the same period. However, the Food Standards Authority in the UK has warned against drawing such conclusions and is launching its own nutrient study.

ALL I WANT FOR CHRISTMAS

According to a BBC programme broadcast in December 2003, this is what the British insist on at Christmas, in order of priority:

1. Turkey and all the trimmings
2. Christmas pudding
3. Sherry trifle
4. Mince pies
5. Roast chicken
6. Baked glazed ham
7. Christmas cake
8. Smoked salmon
9. Turkey sandwiches
10. Roast goose
11. Nut roast

But what did the experts think?

Turkey: 'We eat turkey because it's the biggest thing we can kill. Size matters' – Nigel Slater

Christmas pudding: 'It shouldn't resember a light sponge. It should be like a cannonball' – Keith Floyd

Sherry trifle: 'It's got all the things childhood is made of and then because you're grown-up you add alcohol' – Clarissa Dickson-Wright

Mince pies: 'Mince pies are thing to get plastered with after midnight mass' – Anthony Worrall-Thompson

Roast chicken: 'Who the hell would want to eat roast chicken on Christmas Day?' – Gordon Ramsay

Baked ham: 'Go for the pig's left leg, because it's more tender, as pigs scratch with their right, so that leg is more muscular' – narrator's advice

Christmas cake: 'It's good to have a bit of Christmas

cake to lift your blood sugar when you're running around playing silly games and having too much sex' – Clarissa Dickson-Wright

Smoked salmon: 'It's that feeling of luxury. Even if you eat it as often as I do, it's still a treat' – Clarissa Dickson-Wright

Turkey sandwiches: 'There's no such thing as a good turkey sandwich' – Keith Floyd

Roast goose: 'It should be number one. Comparing a goose to a turkey is like comparing a Bentley Turbo and a Ford Fiesta' – Keith Floyd

EXPERT ADVICE

The secret to perfect fluff

To make sure egg whites go fluffy when you beat them, make sure the bowl and utensils are very clean and absolutely bone-dry. Use a glass, ceramic, stainless steel or copper bowl. Don't use a plastic bowl, as you can't be sure it is spotlessly clean and dry – grease can hide in even small scratches on the surface. A copper bowl is best, as the reaction of egg white and copper makes them lighter, but don't leave them to rest too long in the bowl after beating.

Bring the egg whites to room temperature before you whisk; the colder they are, the longer they take to go fluffy. Use a large bowl to give plenty of room, and a large balloon whisk. If you use an electric mixer, start slowly until the whites turn to foam, then speed up to finish them off. And don't overwhisk, or the foam will collapse and can't be rescued.

JUST TIN TIME

The first tin opener was invented in 1855 – 45 years after the tin was invented.

BUG EATERS ANONYMOUS

Edible bugs and those who eat them...

Australian aborigines eat witchety grubs, Bogong moths, sugar ants and honeypot ants.

Algerians eat desert locusts, cooked in salt water and dried in the sun before eating.

The Japanese eat hachi-no-ko (boiled wasp larvae), zaza-mushi (aquatic insect larvae), inago (fried ricefield grasshoppers), semi (fried cicada) and sangi (fried silk moth pupae). They also enjoy chocolate-dipped ants.

In Kwara State, Nigeria, West Africa, termites, crickets, grasshoppers, caterpillars, palm weevil larvae, and compost beetle larvae are all delicacies.

Ethiopians eat honeycomb containing the larvae.

In Asia and Africa, locusts are said to taste like shrimps and are traditionally eaten with honey.

CULINARY LEGENDS

Marie Antoine Carême (1783-1833) was the founder and architect of French *haute cuisine*. He was one of at least 25 children born to an impoverished family whose father put him out on the street at the age of about 10 to make his own way in the world. Fortunately, he knocked on the door of a restaurant to ask for a job. By the age of 21, he was chef de cuisine to Talleyrand, Louis XVIII's foreign minister. Carême also served as head chef to the future George IV of England, Emperor Alexander I of Russia, and Baron James de Rothschild. He wrote several voluminous works on cookery, which included hundreds of recipes, menus, history of French cookery, instructions for organising kitchens, and instructions for his signature dishes, monumental architectural constructions of food called *pièces montées*. He died at the age of 50, and is remembered as the 'chef of kings and the king of chefs'.

OLD PICTURE, NEW CAPTION

While Hubert always enjoyed his birthday celebrations, he wished that his mother, just once, could have made him a cake shaped like a train

SUMPTUARY LAWS

In times of feasting, governments have occasionally resorted to restricting their citizens from overeating. In ancient Rome, the authorities forbade the eating of very young animals and the slaughter of selected species. They banned displays of luxury and commanded that everyone eat with their doors open, to make it easier for the laws to be enforced. The same tactic was tried in France during the Ancien Regime, when citizens were no longer allowed to serve more than eight courses at dinner, which suggests that the laws were sorely needed.

A HINT OF NOSTALGIA

When a 2004 supermarket poll identified the UK's favourite smells, not surprisingly the top three were food. Smells can influence our behaviour – a poll conducted in 1996 showed that if a store smelled of lavender, ginger, spearmint and orange, the shoppers rated the shop's merchandise more highly.

Fresh bread	21%
Frying bacon	17%
Coffee	13%
Ironing	11%
Cut grass	8%
Babies	7%
The sea	6%
Christmas trees	4%
Perfume	2%
Fish and chips	1%

THAT'S WHY THE COOKIE CRUMBLES

A student from Loughborough University claimed in 2003 to have found the reason why so many biscuits are broken before the packet is opened. While customers assume it is due to rough handling by shop staff, PhD student Qasim Salim thought otherwise and set out to prove a theory. He baked over 100 biscuits during his research, and measured them with laser technology known as digital speckle pattern interferometry. He concluded that when a biscuit cools, it accumulates moisture around the rim, which causes it to expand, but at the same time it loses moisture at the centre, which makes it contract. The opposing forces cause the biscuit to crack. Salim's research supervisor claimed that the findings could be extremely valuable to the £1.5 billion biscuit industry, by reducing waste.

MORE FILMS FOR FOODIES

Alice's Restaurant
Breakfast at Tiffany's
Guess Who's Coming to Dinner
The Spitfire Grill
The Wedding Banquet

AND IT ALL TASTES LIKE CHICKEN

Zoophagy, the practice of eating exotic species of animal for pleasure, was perhaps most memorably practised by Francis Trevelyan Buckland (1826-88). In *Rogues, Villains and Eccentrics*, William Donaldson records that Buckland, a keen amateur naturalist, kept a small menagerie while studying at Oxford University, including a chameleon, an eagle, a jackal, some marmots and a bear named after the king of Assyria. As a small boy he had cooked up squirrel pie and battered mice, but his tastes in adulthood grew more extravagant, stretching, for example, to a panther, which he had sent over from the Surrey Zoological Gardens. Over the years he tried whale, elephant trunk ('rubbery'), rhinoceros pie, porpoise, and a giraffe that had been pre-cooked, thanks to a fire in the giraffe house. A high point in his gastronomic career was perhaps the Eland Dinner, held at the London Tavern in 1859, at which he attempted to persuade his fellow diners that eland should become part of the national diet. We must assume he was not successful, but the assembled company nevertheless enjoyed a menu of sea slug, deer soup and kangaroo.

I'LL HAVE MINE OVER EASY

For those unfamiliar with American English, here's a
quick guide to make sure you don't go hungry:

biscuit – cookie
chick pea – garbanzo bean
chips – French fries
coriander – cilantro (the fresh herb)
cos lettuce – romaine lettuce
hot dog – weenie/wiener
filter coffee – drip coffee
ice lolly – Popsicle

WHAT'S THAT SMELL?

Surströmming may be the world's smelliest food. It is
a fermented herring popular in Sweden, which was first
produced by accident by some dishonest fishermen,
who sold their surplus herring stock (which had begun
to ferment) to some unsuspecting villagers. When they
returned the following year with properly salted herring,
the villagers rejected it and asked for the same as the
previous year. So the fishermen began to create
surströmming especially for them.

The herring are placed in a closed barrel with half the
usual amount of salt needed to preserve them, and the
barrels are left out in the summer sun for some months,
then opened to be repacked and sold. The sale causes
something of a stampede. In *North Atlantic Seafood*,
Alan Davidson records that a fishery official in the area
remembered, as a young man, that when the barrels of
herring were opened, 'birds began to drop dead from the
sky'. The fish is served with chopped red onion, potatoes
and, as Davidson relates, 'thin slices of a special bread,
tunnbröd, which the northerners carry about in their
Wellington boots'.

COOKING CONUNDRUMS

My first is in dill but never in sage
My second's in apple and also greengage
My third is in bread but never in butter
My fourth is in foil but never in cutter
My fifth is in sausage but never in roll
My whole serves your dinner, straight from the bowl
What am I?
Answer on page 144

TEN CARROT FACTS

1. Carrots were first grown as a medicine

2. Carrots were originally purple, red, white, black and yellow

3. Carrots were imported to Europe in the 14th century; Flemish refugees brought them to the UK in the 15th century

4. Orange carrots were bred by the Dutch to match the colours of the House of Orange

5. In James I's time, fashionable ladies wore the flowers and feathery leaves of the carrot in their hair as a decoration

6. Carrot tea made from the leaves is said to be good for gout

7. During World War II, carrots were used to make marmalade and fizzy drinks

8. Jelly beans are made in carrot pie flavour

9. There is as much carrot in four organic carrots as there is in five non-organic carrots

10. Mel Blanc, the voice of Bugs Bunny, didn't like carrots

Given that tea is so firmly associated with England, it is surprising that we were one of the last European countries to taste it. Tea first reached Holland in 1610 and spread to neighbouring countries decades before we got so much as a sniff. The French adopted it with great enthusiasm, although once the novelty had worn off, they returned to their first love, coffee. The first public sale of tea in England was in 1657 and it quickly replaced ale as the national drink, which had a helpful effect on national sobriety. Its popularity was encouraged by Catherine of Braganza, who, when she married Charles II in 1662, brought with her from Portugal a love of tea.

In 1699, England was taking delivery of 40,000lbs; by 1790, we were consuming 18 million lbs of tea a year. But like most popular foodstuffs, it became a target for taxation. At first this was only around a shilling a pound (to pay for the Battle of the Boyne) but by 1773, tax accounted for 64% of its price.

High taxes, of course, encouraged smuggling and the tea tax was constantly being reduced to put the smugglers out of business then raised again when the government ran out of money. Ironically it was the Boston Tea Party that put tea taxes in the UK up to their all-time high of 119% in 1784; the money was needed to quell the American revolution. But soon after, the tax was cut drastically, to end the smuggling once and for all, and tea took its rightful place as the nation's favourite drink.

EDIBLE PLAYS

An Absolute Turkey – Georges Feydeau
The Cherry Orchard – Anton Chekhov
The Cocktail Party – TS Eliot
The Gingerbread Lady – Neil Simon
Icecream – Caryl Churchill
Individual Fruit Pies – Mike Leigh
Table Manners – Alan Ayckbourn
Under Milk Wood – Dylan Thomas

LUCKY FOOD

The origin of some foodie superstitions:

Don't spill the salt – this dates back to the days when salt was expensive, so spilling it was wasteful. Salt is a symbol of friendship and welcome, and salt and bread is still a traditional gesture of welcome in some cultures.

Do spill your wine – an omen of good luck, as it anticipates celebrations.

Bash in your empty eggshell – eggs were once considered mysterious and sacred, and it was thought that magicians used them to cast spells, writing the spell on the inside of the empty eggshell. To crush the eggshell is to crush the evil spell.

Throw rice at weddings – this wishes the couple prosperity and abundance in their married life.

Don't cross knives at table – because it symbolises the cross of crucifixion, and the crossing of swords with your enemy.

Don't have 13 people to dinner – because of the association with the Last Supper. Judas was the 13th man; had he not been there, things might have turned out quite differently.

NEW IN STORE

The explosion of expeditions to the New World (the Americas) in the 16th and 17th centuries introduced new flavours to the European table:

beans – kidney, butter and scarlet runner beans, brought back by Columbus
chillies – brought back by Columbus
chocolate – brought back by Cortés
maize – brought back from Cuba by Columbus
Guinea-fowl – brought by Portuguese from West Africa, around 1530
Jerusalem artichokes – discovered by Champlain in Canada in 1603
pineapples – brought back by Columbus
potatoes – Sir Francis Drake brought the potato back from the Caribbean, where he stopped in 1586
tomatoes – brought back from Mexico in 1519 by Cortés
turkey – brought back from Mexico around 1523 by Levantine or Turkish merchants, hence its name (its Mexican name was *uexolotl*)

The New World also gave us avocados, haricot beans, French beans, peanuts, vanilla, red peppers, green peppers and tapioca.

PEASE PORRIDGE NINE DAYS OLD

Centuries ago, people used to cook in a big pot that always hung over the fire. Every day they lit the fire and added things to the pot. The main ingredient was vegetables. They would eat the stew for dinner, and heat leftovers up again the next day. Sometimes the stew had food in it that had been there for quite a while – hence the rhyme, 'Pease porridge hot, pease porridge cold, pease porridge in the pot nine days old.'

MORE FILMS FOR FOODIES

Almonds and Raisins
Bhaji on the Beach
A Clockwork Orange
Fried Green Tomatoes
Goodbye Mr Chips
Merci Pour Le Chocolat
There's a Girl in My Soup

DANGEROUS FOODS

Bitter almonds contain poisonous prussic acid.

Bitter manioc contains cyanide and is very toxic unless pounded, grated, soaked and heated. In 1981, a water shortage in Mozambique meant that it was not prepared thoroughly and over 1,000 people suffered paralysis after eating it.

Carrots eaten in excess can cause jaundice.

Liver eaten in excess can cause vitamin A overdose and birth defects.

Mochi, a Japanese New Year's food, is traditionally made outdoors by pounding a steamed, glutinous rice with a large wooden mallet until a gummy mass forms. The mochi must be chewed carefully, or it can cause choking when swallowed.

The **Nardoo seeds** used by aboriginals to make cakes are toxic when raw. They were the final meal of explorers Burke and Wills in 1861.

Nutmeg eaten in excess can be hallucinogenic.

Red kidney beans are toxic if inadequately boiled.

Green potatoes are poisonous when raw.

Rhubarb leaves are full of oxalic acid and should never be eaten.

Taro leaves, the leaves of a tropical starchy tuber contain oxalic acid and can only be eaten when well cooked.

OLD PICTURE, NEW CAPTION

Doris discovers the drawbacks to baking double-crust pies.

EXPERT ADVICE

Knives you should have in your cutlery drawer

Boning knife – for removing raw meat from the bone,
and for trimming fat
Bread knife – can also be used to cut cakes and pastries
Carving knife – for the Sunday roast
Cook's knife – for general chopping, slicing and dicing
Filleting knife – for filleting and skinning fish,
and removing membranes from meat
Paring knife – for finer slicing and dicing

Sharpen your knives once or twice a month. To test if
your knife needs sharpening, try it out on a tomato; a
sharp knife will slice through the skin of a tomato with
only the slightest of pressure.

SAY IT WITH FOOD

A little pot is soon hot – a small person is easily riled
Bachelor's fare – bread, cheese and kisses
Baker's knee – knock-knees (because of the
baker's habit of standing all day)
Bread and circuses – free food and entertainment
Cry barley – call a truce (barley is a corruption of 'parley'
and was a cry for truce in a rough game)
Don't roast your coffee beans in the marketplace –
don't tell your secrets to a stranger
Fiddler's pay – meat, drink and money
Ginger group – a small group designed to spice up the
apathetic majority, usually in politics
He eats no fish – someone who is honest and trustworthy
(used in Elizabeth I's time, as protestants refused to adopt
the Roman Catholic custom of eating fish on a Friday)
Hungry dogs will eat dirty pudding – a hungry
person will eat anything
It is time to lay our nuts aside – time to leave off
childish pursuits and become adults
Measure other people's corn by one's own bushel –
judge others using yourself as the standard
Men of the same kidney – of the same disposition
(kidneys were thought to be the seat of affection)
Soft (or fair) words butter no parsnips –
mere words will not get us fed
So that accounts for the milk in the coconut –
said when the cause of something becomes apparent
To make chalk of one and cheese of the other –
to favour one over the other
To take pepper in the nose – to take offence
Tis an old rat that won't eat cheese – only a very
wise or experienced person won't take a juicy bait
With an eye to the loaves and fishes – with an
eye on the material rewards

Bakewell Tart

The small Derbyshire town supposedly has a pudding named after it because of a hapless cook. In the 18th century, the assistant cook at the Rutland Arms Hotel was making strawberry jam tarts. However she put jam at the bottom of the pastry case and then poured butter, eggs and sugar over the top and baked it all. Luckily, the guests loved the new dessert and the recipe has survived. Today, the treat comprises a sweet pastry base, with a red jam and almond filling, covered with a deep layer of white icing. A glacé cherry is then placed on top.

Bath Buns

The first Bath Bun is thought to have been served in the Pump Room in Bath during the 1670s. It is a round, yeasty cake flavoured with mixed spices and lemon and decorated with currants and nibbed sugar. It is baked on top of sugar cubes that soften during baking and are absorbed into the dough, leaving a pattern of neat squares on the bottom and a crunchy texture.

Battenburg Cake

Named in honour of the marriage of Princess Victoria to Prince Louis of Battenburg in 1884, this cake consists of four square lengths of sponge cake, baked in an oblong tin. Two of the lengths are pink and two are yellow and they are stuck together with apricot jam and wrapped in a layer of marzipan.

Black Forest Gateau

The Black Forest area in the south of Germany is known for the quality of its pastries, cakes, and especially for sour cherries. Black Forest Gateau is chocolate cake with cherries and whipped cream.

Brussel Sprouts

The origin of the sprout is unknown but the first mention of them can be traced to the late 16th century. They are thought to be native to the area around Brussels, hence the name. They are now cultivated across Europe and the US.

Cornish Pasties

The pasty originally came about as a handy lunch to be taken down the tin mines by Cornish men. It was practical and yet hardy, the traditional filling being beef and potato, with some onion thrown in for good measure. The pastry case kept it edible while the men were down the mines; and a knob of pastry at one end meant it could be held with dirty hands, then the lump discarded. Tradition has it that original pasties contained meat and vegetables in one end and jam or fruit in the other end.

Coburg Loaf

Queen Victoria's consort, Prince Albert, was responsible for the naming of the Coburg Loaf. This is round and crusty with two slashes on the top. He came from Saxe-Coburg and the loaf was introduced shortly after his marriage to Victoria in 1840.

Madeira Cake

This is a simple sponge cake, often sprinkled with candied lemon peel halfway through baking. It is usually served with a glass of madeira, a fortified wine named after the Portuguese island from where it originated.

Tabasco Sauce

This hot sauce is made from red peppers, vinegar, water and salt and is aged in white oak barrels. It is named after the Tabasco River and the Tabasco State in Mexico, but not the Tabasco pepper, which it does not contain.

Yorkshire Pudding

The traditional accompaniment to the Sunday roast was originally a 'dripping pudding' cooked under the spit on which the beef was cooking so that the meat juices dripped onto it. The 18th century cook Hannah Glasse first gave it the name Yorkshire Pudding.

COOKING CONUNDRUMS

What is an Aktienbolaget gasaccumulator?
Answer on page 144

WHAT'S FOR DINNER, DARLING?

• Susan Barber killed her husband by putting weedkiller in his steak and kidney pie. She was jailed for life in 1982.

• Florence Maybrick killed her husband with arsenic after he beat her for taking a lover (although he had a mistress). She served 15 years of a life-sentence and died in 1941.

• Madeleine Smith poisoned her lover by putting arsenic in his hot chocolate when he broke off their affair. She was acquitted when the defence showed that he was a seducer and a habitual user of arsenic. Smith died in 1928, aged 93.

• Dr Hawley Crippen poisoned his overbearing wife, so he could be with his lover. He was hanged in 1910.

• Adelaide Bartlett was accused in 1886 of poisoning her husband with chloroform after he encouraged her relationship with another man, left her everything in his will, and made her lover the executor. She was acquitted when no one could work out how she'd got him to swallow the chloroform (it burns the throat).

• Mary Ann Cotton killed an unspecified number of people (30 or more) with arsenic, including her second husband, two stepsons and two of her lovers. She was hanged in 1873.

• Margaret Fernseed, prostitute and brothel-keeper, was convicted of the murder of her husband, after it was noted (on finding his dead body) that she had at one time tried to poison him. She was hanged in 1608.

RECORD BREAKERS

If you wonder whether your vegetable patch
is up to scratch, take this list with you when you
next go a-weeding...

Longest beetroot: 5.504m (18ft, 0.6in),
grown in the UK in 2002

Longest carrot: 335cm (132in), grown in the UK in 1987

Longest parsnip: 5m (16ft, 4in) grown in the UK in 2000

Largest bunch of bananas: 473 bananas, grown in
the Canary Islands, 2001

Largest pumpkin: 606.7kg (1,337lb, 9oz), grown in
the USA in 2002

OSBERT'S MARVELLOUS EGG

Sir George Reresby Sitwell (1860-1943), father of the literary trio Osbert, Sacheverell and Edith, was a keen medievalist and inventor and one of England's more entertaining eccentrics. His several sitting rooms were filled with boxes containing notes on monographs yet to be written, such as 'Acorns as an Article of Medieval Diet' and 'My Inventions'. One of these inventions was the Sitwell Egg. Devised as a nourishing and easily transportable meal for travellers, it comprised a 'yolk' of smoked meat and a 'white' of compressed rice contained within a synthetic shell. He presented it to Gordon Selfridge, the founder of Selfridges, but as nothing more was heard of it, we must assume that Mr Selfridge was unimpressed. Which is surprising, given that one of Sir George's rules of life was that he should never be contradicted, as it interfered with the functioning of his gastric juices, and he erected a sign to that effect at his home, Renishaw Hall in Derbyshire, to warn off argumentative visitors.

COOKING CONUNDRUMS

Who had to obtain the apples of Hesperides?
Answer on page 144

CULINARY LEGENDS

Hannah Glasse (1708-1770) was one of the most popular cookbook writers of her time, which was largely the result of good timing. The Puritans had banned spices and frowned upon rich food, and the end of Puritanism was the beginning of a passion for good food. Hannah's first book, *The Art of Cookery Made Plain and Easy* (1747) was aimed at the inexperienced cook and not the professional chef. 'I only hope my Book will answer the Ends I intend it for,' wrote Hannah in her introduction, 'which is to improve the Servants, and save the Ladies a great deal of Trouble'. She further believed that 'every servant who can but read will be capable of making a tolerable good Cook'.

Hannah scorned French cookery as fanciful, but cheerfully plagiarised French recipes – copyright was a tenuous idea at the time, and most cookbook writers shamelessly lifted recipes from each other. Samuel Johnson thought that her book must have been written by a man, which was the usual case at the time, 'because women can spin very well, but they cannot make a good book of cookery'. Cookbooks, indeed, were often written by chefs for other chefs, and were hard for ordinary men and women to understand. Glasse presented her recipes plainly and clearly, and assumed that her book would be bought by employers to give to their servants.

She also wrote the *Servant's Directory* and *The Compleat Confectioner*, published in 1770, the year of her death.

OLD PICTURE, NEW CAPTION

*Dr Prendergast demonstrates the benefits
of a vitamin-enriched diet*

WE WOULD LIKE TO THANK...

A few small culinary inventions that changed the way we
eat – though not all of them for the better...

Invention	By	Date
Solid chocolate	Francois-Louis Cailler	1819
Doughnut with hole	Hanson Gregory	1847
Chewing-gum	John Curtis	1848
Potato crisps	George Crum	1853
Condensed milk	Gail Borden	1856
Vending machine	Percival Everitt	1883
Coca-Cola	Dr John Pemberton	1886
Vacuum flask	James Dewar	1892
Ice cream cones	Italo Marcioni	1896
Instant coffee	Nestlé	1937
Food processor	Kenneth Wood	1947
Non-stick pan	Marc Gregoir	1954

COOKING CONUNDRUMS

The answers. As if you needed them.

P6.   Take the fruit from the box marked 'apples and oranges'. If it's an apple, then that box must be the 'apples' box; the box marked 'apples' must contain oranges, and the remaining box both apples and oranges. The opposite is true if you take out an orange.

P11.   In *The Merry Wives of Windsor* Bardolph calls Slender a 'Banbury cheese'.

P22.   People (it's another word for cannibal)

P37.   A snake

P41.   It is a derivation of the French *fouler*, to crush

P57.   Onion

P77.   Seven eggs. The first person bought one half of his eggs plus one half an egg (4 eggs) This left him three eggs. The second person bought one-half of his eggs plus one. half an egg, (2 eggs) leaving the man one egg. The last person bought one-half of his eggs plus one-half an egg, (1 egg) leaving no eggs.

P83.   The *Association Amicale des Amateurs d'Authentiques Andouilletes*, dedicated to andouillettes, a type of pork sausage.

P86.   16 inches. Volumes One and 10 remain unmunched.

P97.   An ear of corn

P103.   An onion

P115.   They're champagne bottle sizes, of which Balthazar (16 bottles) is the largest, a Methuselah contains eight and a Salmanazar 12.

P120.   An egg

P131.   Ladle

P140.   The full, original name of the Aga stove.

P142.   Hercules, as one of his 12 tasks of penitence.

BIBLIOGRAPHY

The A-Z of Almost Everything, Trevor Montague

The Atlas of Food, Erik Millstone and Tim Lang

Brewer's Rogues, Villains and Eccentrics,
William Donaldson

Brewer's Phrase and Fable

The Chocolate Book, Helge Rubinstein

The Devil's Cup, Stewart Lee Allen

Feast: A History of Grand Eating, Roy Strong

Food, Clarissa Dickson-Wright

Food: An Oxford Anthology, Brigid Allen

Food in History, Reay Tannahill

The Good Web Guide: Food, Jenni Muir

A History of Britain, Simon Schama

Hungry for You, Joan Smith

In The Devil's Garden, Stewart Lee Allen

It Must've Been Something I Ate, Jeffrey Steingarten

Larousse Gastronomique

Leith's Techniques Bible, Susan Spaull and Lucinda
Bruce-Gardyne

The Little Food Book, Craig Sams

Food: A History, Felipe Fernández-Armesto

The Oxford Companion to the English Language,
Tom McArthur

The Physiology of Taste, Jean Anthelme Brillat-Savarin

A Social History of England, Asa Briggs

Superfoods, Michael Van Straten

The Top Ten of Everything 2004, Russell Ash

The Victory Cookbook, Marguerite Patten

COOKING NOTES, JOTTINGS, IDEAS AND DOODLES

COOKING NOTES, JOTTINGS,
IDEAS AND DOODLES

**COOKING NOTES, JOTTINGS,
IDEAS AND DOODLES**

COOKING NOTES, JOTTINGS, IDEAS AND DOODLES

COOKING NOTES, JOTTINGS, IDEAS AND DOODLES

COOKING NOTES, JOTTINGS, IDEAS AND DOODLES

COOKING NOTES, JOTTINGS, IDEAS AND DOODLES

COOKING NOTES, JOTTINGS, IDEAS AND DOODLES

COOKING NOTES, JOTTINGS, IDEAS AND DOODLES

COOKING NOTES, JOTTINGS, IDEAS AND DOODLES

**COOKING NOTES, JOTTINGS,
IDEAS AND DOODLES**

COOKING NOTES, JOTTINGS,
IDEAS AND DOODLES

COOKING NOTES, JOTTINGS, IDEAS AND DOODLES